Making Posh Paws and his Prehistoric Friends

Making Posh Paws and his Prehistoric Friends

Jane Gisby

All patterns full-size, ready to trace

Scaled from the approved large toy animals in the 'Story of the Earth' exhibition in the Geological Museum, London

Mills & Boon Ltd,
London · Sydney · Toronto

First published 1978
Patterns © Jane Gisby 1975. Posh Paws
Regd. Trade Mark.
Multi-Coloured Swap Shop © BBC
Enterprises 1977

ISBN 0 263 06379 8

Typeset by Reproduction Drawings Ltd, Sutton, Surrey
Printed in Great Britain by
A. Wheaton & Co. Ltd, Exeter
for the Publishers Mills & Boon Ltd,
17–19 Foley Street London W1A 1DR

ACKNOWLEDGEMENT

I would like to thank my family
and also the staff at the Geological
Museum and the BBC for their help
and encouragement.

Contents

Introduction

The patterns of the prehistoric creatures in this book are based on an exclusive series designed at a scale of 1in to 1ft by Jane Gisby for the London Geological Museum Exhibition *'The Story of the Earth'*.

While making very attractive toys they are correctly shaped anatomically and the technical notes and artists impressions have been provided by the Museum Staff so that, besides being a range of unusual but well-known creatures to make up, the models, notes and illustrations are collectively very suitable for school projects.

The first dinosaurs that Jane Gisby made were included in the Design Centre Index some years ago and have proved to be very popular indeed. Because so many visitors to the Geological Museum asked for the patterns she agreed to publish some of them, for sale through the Museum Shop.

Many of the models, particularly the Tyrannosaurus Rex ('Posh Paws'), Iguanodon ('Fred'), Triceratops, Woolly Mammoth and Plesiosaur will be instantly recognised from their regular appearances on the very successful BBC TV children's programme 'Multi-Coloured Swap Shop.'

Hints and Instructions

Many books have been written about making soft toys, and most needlewomen and toy makers have their own ideas and special knowledge learnt through long experience. But I hope that I as a professional toy maker may be able to give some hints for anyone making up a soft toy for the first time and in doing so improve their chances of being pleased with their models and encouraged to go on to make some more.

Choice of toy to make

It is always advisable to begin with something fairly simple and only attempt a more ambitious model after some practice. The Ichthyosaur is the easiest to make, and the Pteranodon is probably the most demanding because of the extraordinary shape and dimensions of his wings, which need wiring for support.

Patterns

All the original models that I made for the Museum are in reasonable proportion to each other and this was one reason why they were acceptable. I think that this matter of scale is important and indeed it is rather odd that many artist's impressions of these creatures seem to be approximately the same size—which can be very misleading.

The toys in this book, though based carefully on the Museum designs, are only intended as convenient sizes for making up by people with a reasonable skill, but no more. However they can be made larger or smaller quite easily so that they can be in correct proportion to each other if so required. The 'standard' sizes in the book are quite large enough for most purposes.

Size

If you wish to make large creatures then you will have to give some attention to the use of a really strong wired frame to hold the limbs in appropriate attitudes. The cost and difficulty of completing the toys increase rapidly with size and while these big models do look very impressive they are expensive in materials and time and are hard work to complete. My largest brontosaur needed over 28lbs (12kg) of stuffing and is nearly 7ft (2m) from nose to tail and was made from a scaled-up pattern of the design in this book. If you wish to scale the creatures to a smaller size then you may have trouble with the turning and stuffing of the smaller limbs, particularly the tails, tusks and forepaws.

Materials

Nobody really knows the colour and texture of any of these prehistoric creatures' skins but it is assumed that most of them had scaly, leathery body coverings that blended with their backgrounds rather like crocodiles and rhinoceros. Obviously the Woolly Mammoth was covered with a very shaggy fur, from which he got his name, and these creatures have been found, well preserved, in the Siberian ice.

As a toy maker you can have a lot of fun using remnants to make very original and colourful creatures—and who is to say that these animals did not roam the countryside in skins of various bright colours? Any smooth fabric is suitable providing that it has a firm weave and does not fray easily. A material that is too thin will show the stuffing or filling very easily and a thick material will not give a neat outline when small parts are turned to the right side.

Felt is used for the accessories such as eye backings and for feet. Smaller toys are made out of it entirely. Fur fabric has to be used for the Wooly Mammoth of course, and short pile fabric is satisfactory for other dinosaurs and it does cover small mistakes better than a smooth fabric!

Remember that most fabrics stretch so that the finished toy will be slightly larger than the pattern pieces, this happens particularly with materials that have a large amount of 'give' in one direction.

Finished appearance

There is no reason why your finished toy should look exactly like the illustration which accompanies each set of instructions. The materials can be different and so can the expressions, and the attitudes of the limbs—especially the head and neck. For example a slight angle on the latter and an upward curve to the mouth line can give a most appealing and quizzical look.

Turnings

The patterns in the book are printed without turnings. When you have made your set of pattern templates and chalked their outlines on to material then you have your sewing lines. The turnings must be allowed for before cutting the pieces out. The allowance required will depend on the fabric and the following are recommended:

Pile fur fabrics and easily frayed materials $\frac{5}{8}$in (1.5cm)

Smooth fabrics $\frac{1}{4}$in (0.6cm)

Felts and non-fraying materials when stitched on the outside $\frac{1}{8}$in (0.3cm)

If in doubt leave at least $\frac{3}{4}$ins (1.9 cm) and trim seams after sewing.

Making patterns

REQUIRED: Soft pencil, tracing paper (ordinary grease-proof paper from the kitchen is quite suitable) thin card, paper glue.

If you wish to make a different size of animal you will also need a ruler, set square and rubber. Please see below the separate instructions for scaling.

Paper is not kind to good sharp scissors and therefore it is best to use an old pair to cut out the paper and card. A large envelope or polythene bag is invaluable to hold the various pattern cards once they are cut out, to avoid losing them and having to make more.

METHOD: Lay the tracing paper on to each outline of the animal in turn and mark in the shape with the pencil, taking care with the larger items (that spread over several pages) to line up the start of one part of a shape with the ending of the previous part. The patterns have been drawn out to full size already and the various pieces fit together extremely easily at straight line interfaces which have triangles on them. See Fig. 1.

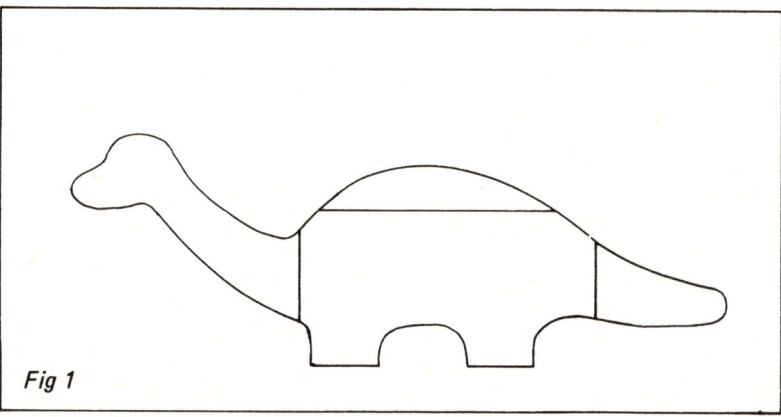

Fig 1

Draw in the straight lines with a ruler as they are invaluable for aligning the next section. Each piece should be a reasonable fit to its neighbour. Mark the triangles for the piece that you have just traced and then look for the next piece that also carries these triangles, align the straight edges, taking care that the triangles correspond and then trace the next part of the shape. Repeat this process for all the patterns for the creature.

Cut out the traced pieces very roughly, and glue them to the card, ensuring that there are no wrinkles in the paper, which will cause errors.

When the glue has dried, carefully cut round the pencil lines to form the pattern templates.

Using each pattern template in turn, cut out sufficient pattern shapes in card to make the complete toy, i.e. two body shapes, eight feet etc. as indicated on the pattern for each creature. Mark each piece with 'right' and 'wrong' as many pieces such as body shapes have to be reversed in order to make complimentary pairs on a fabric which has a pattern on one surface only. See Fig. 2.

On the right side of each template also indicate if turnings are to

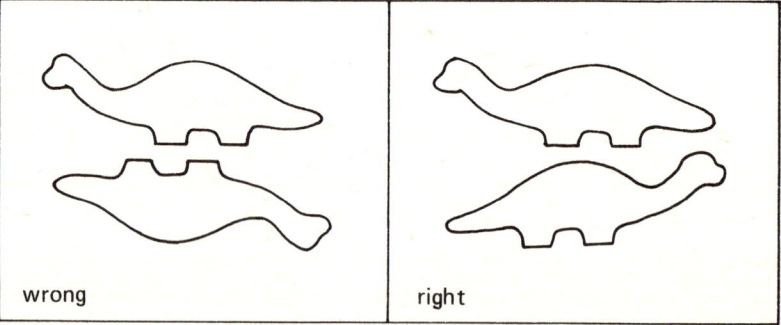

wrong   right

Fig 2

8

be allowed, the direction of the pile (if appropriate) and all sewing marks as shown on the patterns.

Cutting out fabric

REQUIRED: tailor's chalk, soft pencil, cutting-out scissors, pinking shears (optional).

METHOD: Lay out the pattern templates on the material for maximum economy, pin the cards to the 'wrong' side of the fabric and mark around the edges of each. Do not forget to allow for the turnings and the direction of the pile as shown on the patterns. Remember to reverse one side of a body to make a pair.

Remove the cards and cut out, leaving turnings where necessary (note the chalk line is the *sewing line*). The feet and hands are all made from two felt shapes stitched together. It is easier to sew them if only one shape is cut out, the other being roughly cut to size and trimmed to shape when sewn (Fig. 3). Chalk all sewing marks on to the fabric.

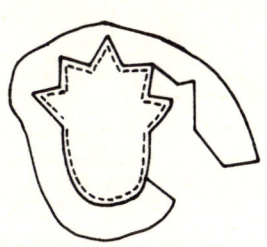

Fig 3

Fur fabric is always cut on the smooth or wrong side with the point of the scissors kept between the pile and the woven backing to avoid cutting the pile. Take care not to lose any of the pieces as they are cut or you may inadvertently throw away some with your scraps.

To make up

REQUIRED: Long steel pins. A long darning and a sewing needle. A toy-maker's curved needle and hat pins are useful; thimble; sewing cottons and thread in appropriate colours; fine darning wools for making features; safety eyes if used; sewing machine (optional but a machine does give a better line on long seams.).

METHOD: See individual instructions for each pattern. It is recommended that all body seams except foot circles and leg arcs are double stitched—one line of machine stitch is made on the sewing line and another line is made $\frac{1}{8}$in (0.3 cm) outside it. The extra strength prevents the sadness and annoyance of a seam giving way just when the last of the stuffing is being put in place. If the whole toy is to be made by hand then a single line of back stitch with a double thread is sufficient and just as strong. When sewing is completed, trim seams, clip to curves before turning.

Count all pins used in fur fabric, and any long darning needles etc. used to hold parts while sewing so that none are left in the fabric.

The following short notes may be useful:

Stay Stitching: This prevents a curved edge from stretching before it is sewn. Make a line of stitches $\frac{1}{8}$in (0.3 cm) outside the seam line.

back stitch

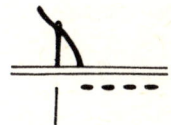

stab stitch

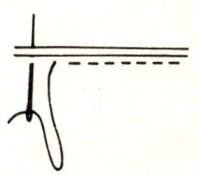

ladder stitch

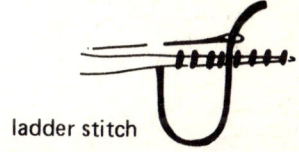

stem stitch

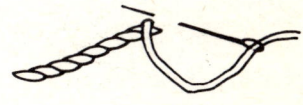

oversewing

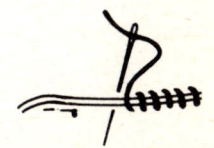

9

satin stitch

Leg Arcs: These darts are essential if a toy is to stand. Right sides together, fold the leg along the straight guide line and stitch along the curved line on the wrong side of the fabric. (Fig. 4).

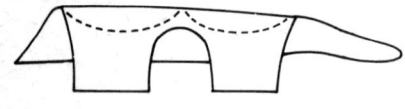

Fig 4

Leg Circles: For toys made in a material that frays, the leg circles are stitched by hand using back stitch and working on the seam line. For felt toys the circles can be trimmed to size and oversewn. (Fig. 5).

Fig 5

Fur Fabric: This material is over sewn at the edges on the wrong side to prevent it slipping when the seams are sewn.

Eyes

Plastic safety eyes make a toy look very alive, especially if used with an eye backing of a contrasting felt. Make a small hole in the eye backing and the body fabric. Place the eye backing in the correct position on the outside of the body fabric and insert the stem of the eye. This is secured by a metal washer which may be either a type to be pushed on by hand or need a fixing tool to press into position. Remember that once the washer is even half way onto the plastic stem it is impossible to remove it. If you are not confident about getting the plastic eyes level then make eyes from felt when the creature is completed. A small bead or button could be used for an eye if the creature is *not* intended for a young child. The placement lines on the patterns are given as guides only. Great fun can be had by altering the expression of a creature by changing the slant of an eye very slightly.

Stuffing

REQUIRED: Synthetic fillings, kapok or scraps. A stuffing stick made from a blunt length of dowling rod or a wooden spoon handle is very useful for placing small amounts of filling in the ends of tails etc.
METHOD: In general insert only small amounts of filling at a time and mould each part of the model as you fill it. The filling must be firm and fill the 'skin' smoothly, but do not force the stuffing in hard or you will simply break your stitching or distort the material by stretching it and the result will be an unsightly bulge.

When stuffing any toy, care should be taken to eliminate all hollows and lumps as they occur, as once the stuffing is completed the only way to correct such mistakes is to take all the filling out and start again.

Stiffening

All the patterns are designed to stand without wire stiffening and will do so if the stuffing of the body, legs and tail is firm and smooth. However if a model is to stand for a long time an arch of wire can be placed in the legs, neck etc. as necessary before stuffing is completed. The Pteranodon of course needs carefully wiring to support the length of the wings.

In all cases ordinary galvanized fencing wire is adequate. The ends must be turned back on themselves and then bound with strips of material to prevent any sharp edges causing accidents. For really large animals, scaled up from the patterns, a stiffening framework is necessary, joined in the body as a type of 'chassis' and for this it is advisable to use mild steel strip.

Finishing

REQUIRED: Fabric adhesive, small brush or pieces of dry foam sponge. METHOD: Complete the model by glueing any small accessories in place. Mouths are embroidered in a single line of stem stitch and the nostrils marked with a few satin stitches.

Brush the toy thoroughly to remove excess stuffing, loose threads etc. Felt should always be brushed with a piece of dry foam sponge as this does not disturb the surface of the fabric. Foam is extremely good for brushing off kapok.

Scaling

If you decide to make a different size of model there are several ways in which you can alter the patterns. However it is important to realise that a small change in each of the three dimensions of length, width and height causes a surprising change in overall size. This is because the changes are multiplied together so that if you double each dimension the creatures makes up eight times as large—which can be quite startling!

For a small change in size you can simply increase or decrease the existing pattern lines by up to $\frac{1}{4}$in (0.6cm) on all the pieces and make up as before. These alterations will cause a surprising change overall, small as they are.

If you wish to make bigger alterations then you must make up a simple grid to produce the new

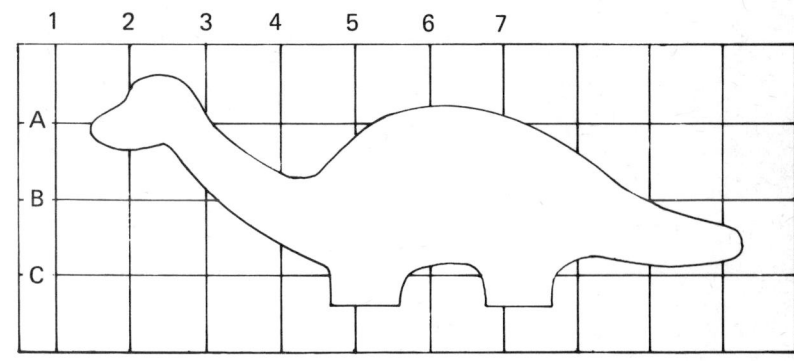

Fig 6

pattern size as described in the following paragraphs. Alternatively you can use a pantograph which can be bought very cheaply if your children do not have one already. They are easy to use and give surprisingly accurate results with only a little practice.

To make the grid, first draw the completed standard pattern in the normal way. Surround this with an accurately drawn rectangle and mark divisions every $\frac{1}{2}$in (1.25cm) along all four sides. Draw in lines to join the corresponding marks across the pattern and number the vertical and letter the horizontal lines (Fig. 6).

Next draw a second accurate rectangle the size of which will depend on the proposed size of the new pattern. If you want a model twice as large then the rectangle and its grid must be twice the size, i.e. 1in (2.5cm) spacings. Similarly to make it half size then the rectangle and grid will be half as large and the grid lines at $\frac{1}{4}$in (0.6cm) spacings. Number the vertical and letter the horizontal lines as before on the standard pattern.

All you need now do is to mark in the positions on the new grid where the pattern lines will cross the grid lines. These positions will of course correspond to, and can be measured from, the same positions on the standard grid and pattern. You can estimate them, measure them, or use a pair of scaling dividers if you are familiar with these instruments. You may find it necessary to add extra grid lines where the curves are rather sharp in order to obtain a good copy of the original shape. Provided that you keep the spacing of the grid lines proportional in the standard and your new grid, you can of course mark in as many or as few as you think you need to achieve a good result. Do not try to be economical with them or your pattern or model will suffer.

When you have enough points marked then join them up with a smooth line to form the outline of the pattern piece at the required new size. Repeat the process for all the other parts that you require.

THE ANIMALS

Brontosaurus: 'Thunder-Lizard'

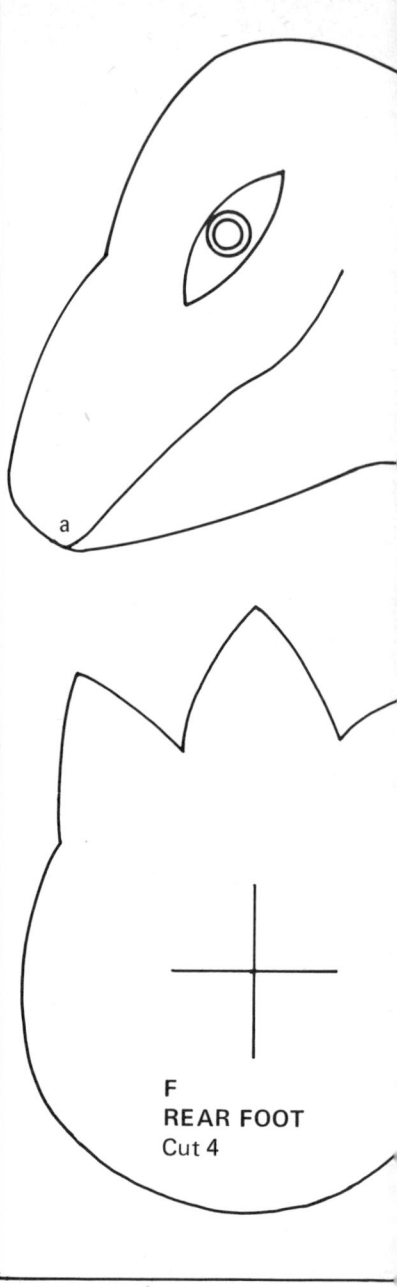

**F
REAR FOOT
Cut 4**

Brontosaurus (thunder-lizard) was a massive plant-eating dinosaur that lived in North America and Europe during the Jurassic Period, 150 million years ago. Brontosaurus was 60 feet (18m) long and weighed 20 tons (200kg), making it one of the largest animals ever to walk on the land. It was about the same length and weight as two double decker buses. The enormous body was supported on four pillar-like legs, while the animal's long neck allowed it to browse on all but the tallest trees. Its small teeth and weak jaws were adapted to eat only soft plant material, and Brontosaurus probably spent much of its time standing in the waters of lakes or swamps eating the Jurassic pondweed. It must have been a ponderous and slow-moving animal whose only hope of escape from a hungry meat-eater was to wade into deep water as fast as possible. Its brain was small so its intelligence was extremely limited.

MATERIALS REQUIRED

Main body fabric: 36 x 36ins (90 x 90cm)
Contrast felt: 12 x 8ins (30 x 20 cm)
One pair plastic safety eyes, 10mm (optional) or scraps of black and white felt
Sewing cotton
Stuffing: 1lb 8oz (0.6kg)
Size of Model: Length 25ins (62 cm); Height 10ins (25cm)

MAKING-UP

Patterns

Make up patterns as explained in Hints and Instructions. Pattern shapes required are: 2 main bodies (A); 2 under-bodies (B); 1 chin gusset (C); 4 leg circles (D); 4 front feet (E); 4 rear feet (F); 2 eye backings (G).

Cutting-out

Place pattern pieces on the fabrics. Two main bodies, 2 under-bodies, 1 chin gusset, 4 leg circles on main body fabric. Four front feet; 4 rear feet; 2 eye backings on contrast felt.

Sewing

*Make a line of stitching along the neck from mouth 'a' to lower neck 'c' (Fig. 1).

*With right sides of fabric together match main body sections. Pin and stitch from 'a' at mouth along the top of the head, neck, back and upper tail to 'e'.

*With right sides together join

Fig 1

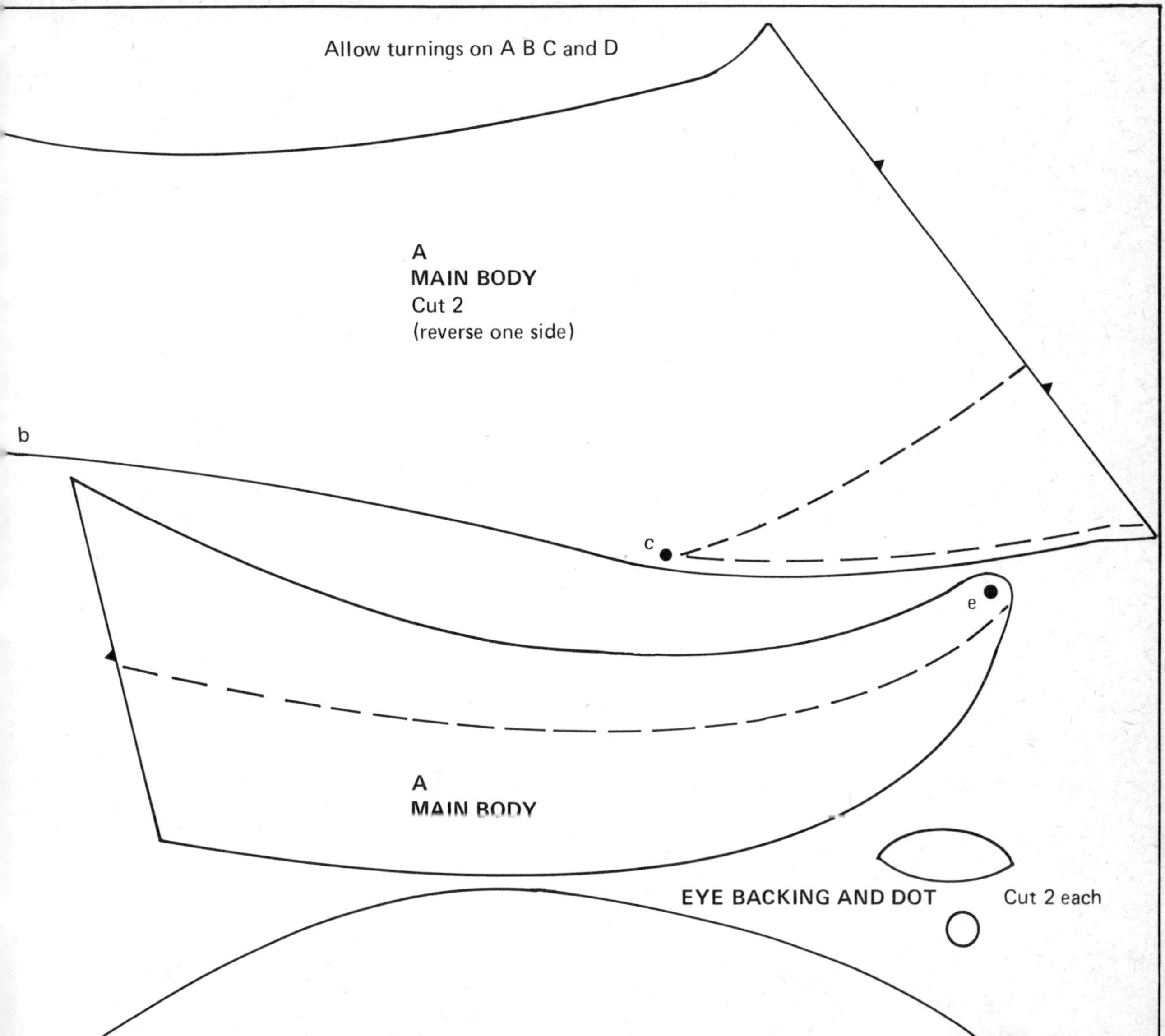

Allow turnings on A B C and D

A
MAIN BODY
Cut 2
(reverse one side)

b

c

e

A
MAIN BODY

A
MAIN BODY

EYE BACKING AND DOT   Cut 2 each

A
MAIN BODY

chin gusset to both sides of head from 'a' at mouth to 'b', breaking stitching at 'a' and 'b' (Fig. 2).

*If plastic eyes are to be used then turn head to right side, smooth the centre seam flat between finger and thumb, pin eye backing in position and fix eye as explained in Hints and Instructions.

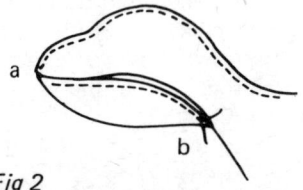

Fig 2

*Make leg arcs on wrong side of each under-body leg by folding along centre lines and stitching on the curved lines (Fig. 3).

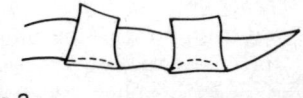

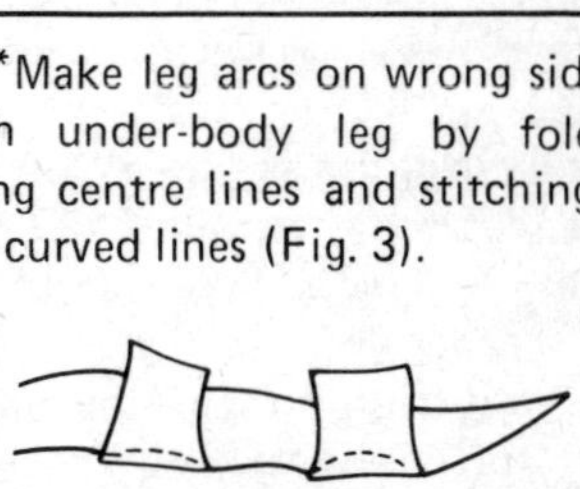

Fig 3

*With right sides together stitch under-bodies together along centre seam leaving open gap for stuffing.

*With right sides together match and pin underbodies to main body.

*Stitch together neck from end of chin gusset 'b' to join of under-bodies 'c'.

*Stitch under-bodies to main bodies from 'c' at neck to 'e' at tail leaving open ends of legs.

*With right sides together insert leg circles and back stitch by hand into place (Fig. 4).

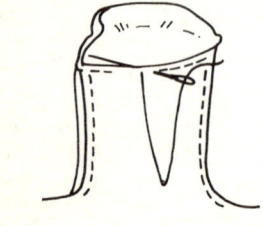

Fig 4

*Check that no pins are left in the fabric. Turn the Brontosaurus to the right side. Ease out the head and tail with the stuffing stick.

Stuffing

*Begin by filling the head and neck with stuffing. Work with small amounts at a time and put it into position with the blunt stick. The shape of the head should be moulded by filling out the jaws. Place sufficient filling between the stems of the plastic eyes. The neck and tail must be firmly stuffed to retain their shape. Larger amounts of stuffing can be put into the body, moulding it into the back 'hump'. When the body is partly filled the legs are stuffed. The stuffing should be moulded into the top of the legs to indicate a heaviness at the thighs. A wire arch can be placed into each pair of legs but this is not essential provided that sufficient stuffing is used to achieve a firm outline. Complete the body filling and close the gap. Depending on the type of material and the amount of stuffing used it may be necessary to make two small tucks in the fabric to obtain a smooth straight closing. Brush the model to remove excess filling.

Feet

*Make up the feet by pinning two rear foot shapes (three-toed) and two front foot shapes (single-toes). Top stitch each pair together. Make up two other feet the same way. Cut a small slit in the top fabric of each foot and insert a little stuffing. The slits will be covered

A MAIN BODY

Leave open to stuff

B UNDER-BODY Indicated by dotted lines inside A
Cut 2
(reverse one side)

Leg arcs
(Under-body only)

D LEG CIRCL
Cut 4

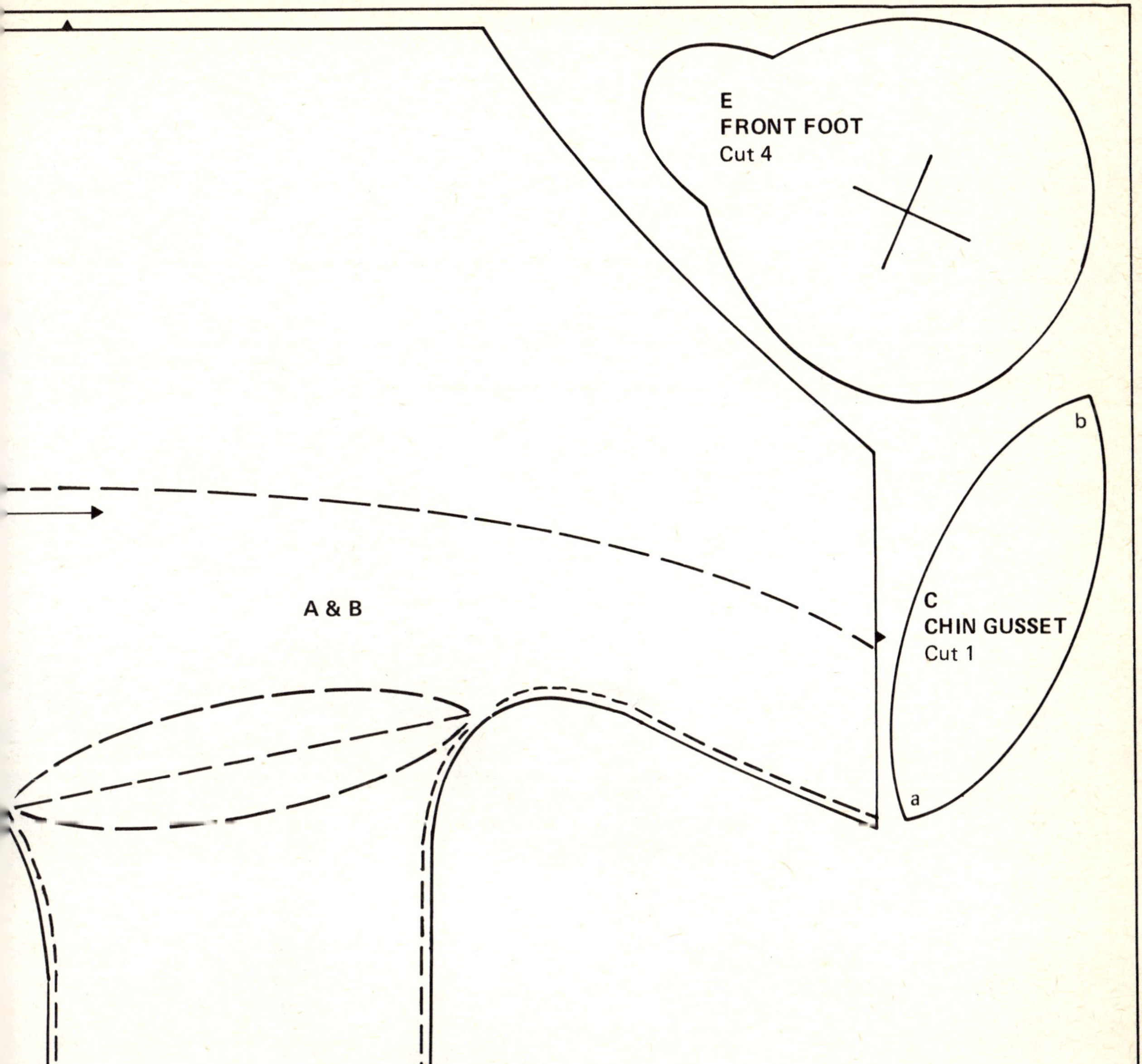

**E
FRONT FOOT
Cut 4**

b

**C
CHIN GUSSET
Cut 1**

a

A & B

by the ends of the legs (Fig. 5).

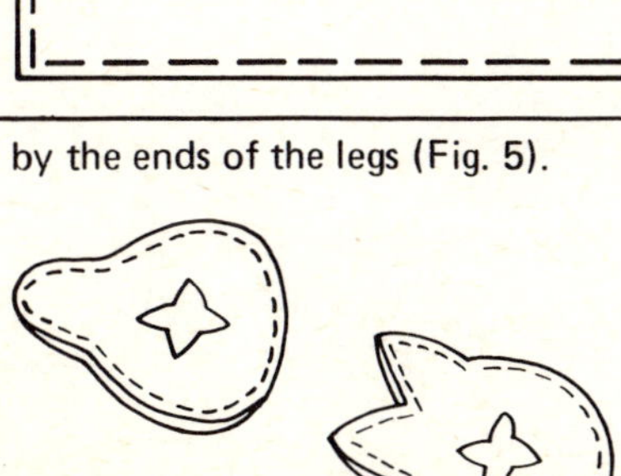

*The feet are now slip-stitched on to the ends of the legs (Fig. 6).

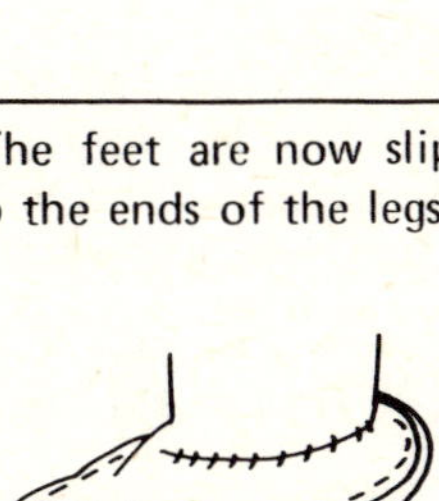

Finishing

*Make the eyes, if plastic ones have not been used. Eyes can be cut as two small circles from a scrap of felt, sewn on to the eye backing and stitched to the head (Fig. 7). Embroider a line of chain stitching to indicate the 'smile' and

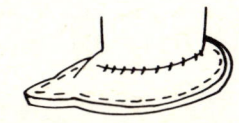

Fig 5

Fig 6

M.P.P.—B

17

add a few more chain stitches to
mark the nostrils.

Fig 7

Dimetrodon: Sail-Back Lizard

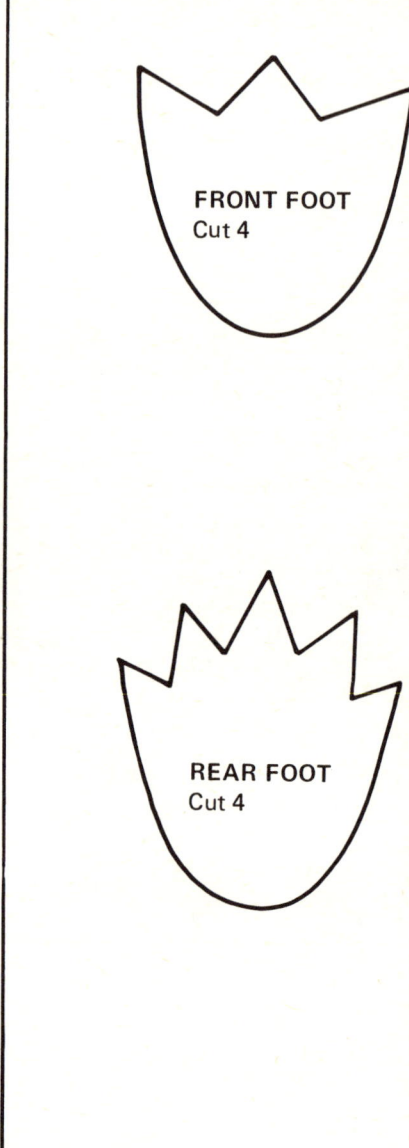

FRONT FOOT
Cut 4

REAR FOOT
Cut 4

Dimetrodon, the sail-backed reptile, lived in North America during the Permian Period, 250 million years ago. It was one of the earliest of the reptiles and lived at a time when dinosaurs, birds and mammals had not yet evolved. A great desert covered much of America and Europe at this time. Dimetrodon belonged to a group called the mammal-like reptiles, even though it was cold-blooded and laid eggs just like a crocodile. This was the group from which the mammals like you and me eventually evolved. Dimetrodon was about twelve feet (3.5m) long and, having sharp dagger-like teeth, must have been a ferocious meat-eater. The enormous 'sail', formed by a flap of skin supported on bony extensions of the backbone, seems to have been used to regulate body temperature, allowing the animal to keep warm on a cold day and cool on a hot one.

MATERIALS REQUIRED

Main body fabric—felt: 18 x 18ins (45 x 45cm)

Contrast felt for sails etc: 12 x 18ins (30 x 45cm)

Plastic safety eyes or scrap of white felt: 8mm

Black and white embroidery cottons or fine wools

Florist's or other thin pliable wire: 4ft (1.2m)

Sewing cotton

Stuffing: 6oz (169g)

Size of model: Length 16ins (40 cm); Height 8ins (20cm)

Note: The Dimetrodon should be rather smaller than this compared to the other models.

MAKING-UP

Patterns

Make up patterns as explained in Hints and Instructions. Pieces required are: 2 main bodies (A); 1 under-body (B); 2 inner front legs (C); 2 inner rear legs (D); 4 leg circles (E); 2 eye lids (F); 4 front foot shapes (G); 4 rear foot shapes (H); 2 sail fins (I); 2 eye backings (J).

Cutting-out

Place pattern pieces on the fabrics. Two main bodies; 1 under-body; 2 inner front legs and rear legs; 4 leg circles and 2 eye lids all on main body fabric. Four front foot shapes; 4 rear foot shapes; 2 sail fins and 2 eye backings on contrast felt. Cut out all shapes except one side of the sail which is left with extra fabric around the edge for ease when sewing (Fig. 7).

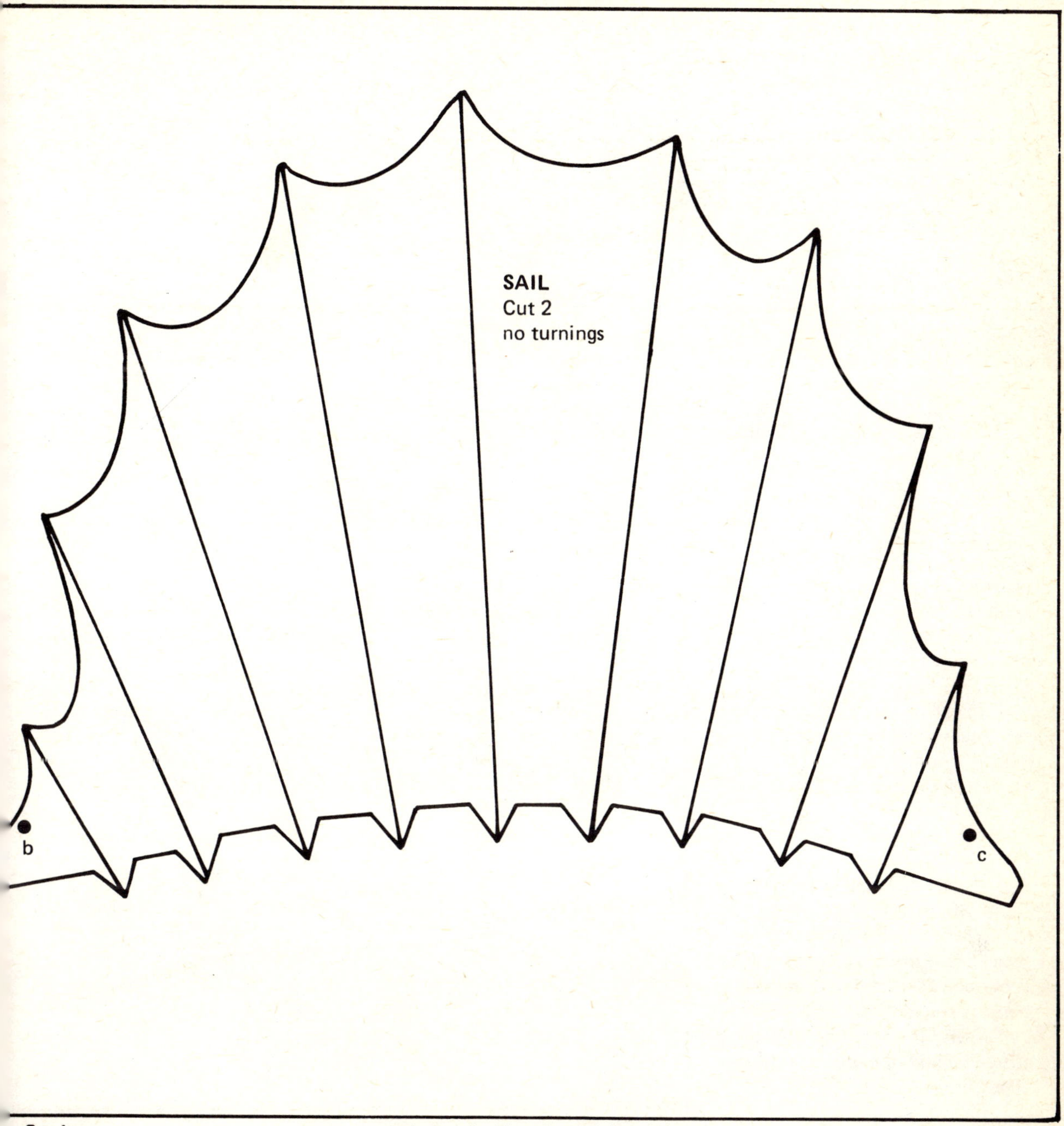

SAIL
Cut 2
no turnings

● b

● c

Sewing

Body

*With right sides together pin both main body shapes together. Stitch with a $\frac{1}{4}$in (0.6cm) seam or oversewing on the wrong side— from 'a' at mouth to 'b' on back, leave open 'b' to 'c' for sail and

continue stitching from 'c' to 'd' at end of tail (Fig. 1).

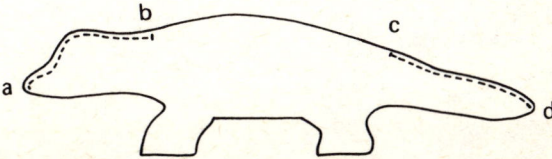

Fig 1

*If plastic eyes are to be used, turn head to right side and fix the eye and backing as explained in Hints and Instructions.

*With right sides together stitch front and rear inner legs to under-body between dots, matching letters 'e' and 'f' (Fig. 2).

*Right sides together pin under-body to main body. Stitch on both sides from head around legs to end of tail, leaving open ends of legs and breaking stitching at 'a' and 'd' (Fig. 3).

*Turn Dimetrodon to right side out.

*Trim foot circles to fit ends of legs and oversew into place (Fig. 4).

Sail fin

Note: Stitch the sail fin by machine or stab-stitch. The ribs can be marked very lightly using a soft pencil and a ruler.

*Pin the cut-out sail shape to the roughly cut-out contrast felt (Fig. 7).

*On each rib marked on the pattern make a double line of stitching which is taken to a point at the scalloped edge to form a channel for the wire (Fig. 5).

*Work from the centre rib to the outsides. It is recommended that a trial channel of stitching is made on some scrap felt and a wire inserted to make sure that the distance between the rows of stitching is correct. It should be as narrow as possible (Fig. 6).

*When all ribs are completed stitch around the upper scalloped edge of sail.

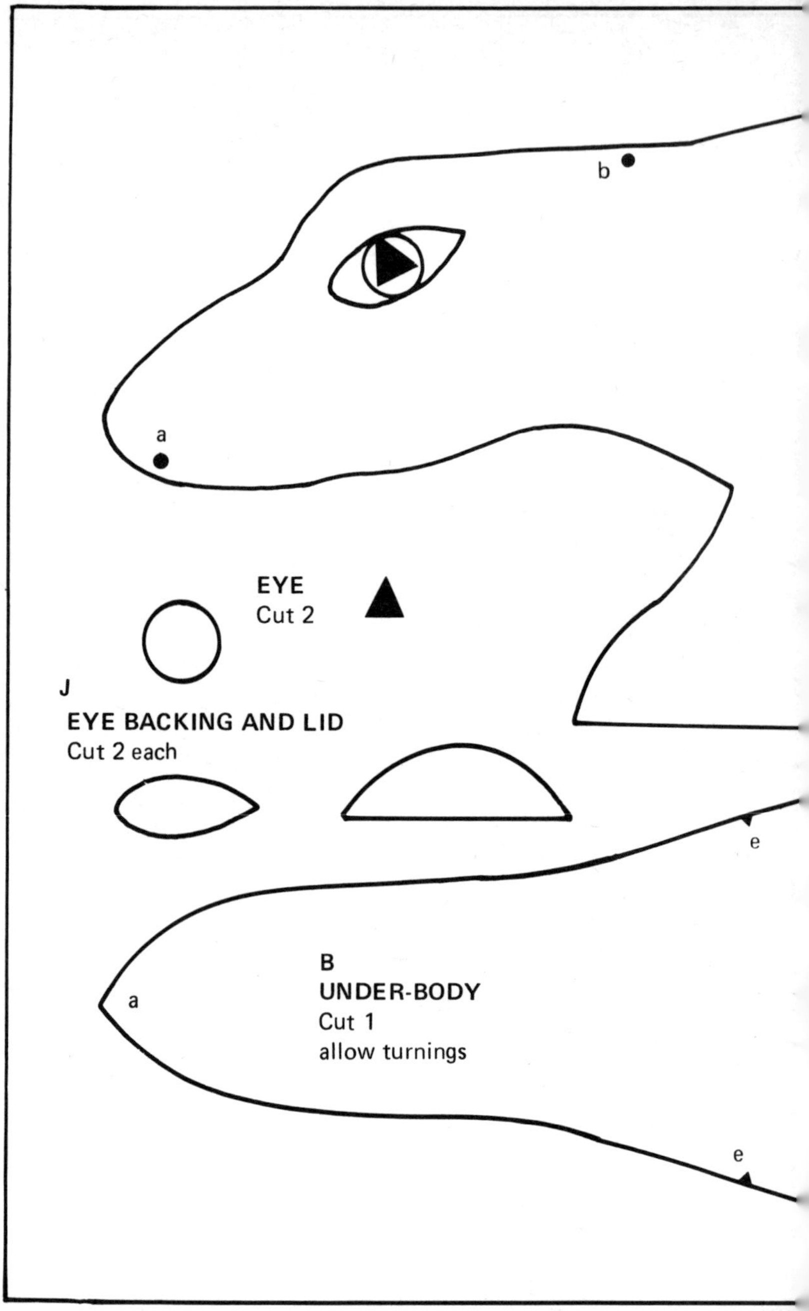

b •

a
•

EYE
Cut 2 ▲

J
EYE BACKING AND LID
Cut 2 each

e

B
UNDER-BODY
Cut 1
allow turnings

a

e

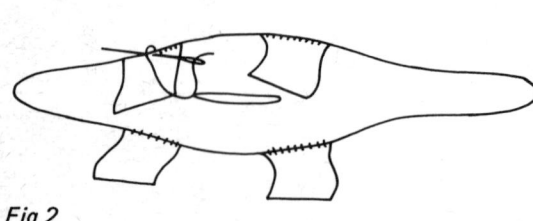

Fig 2

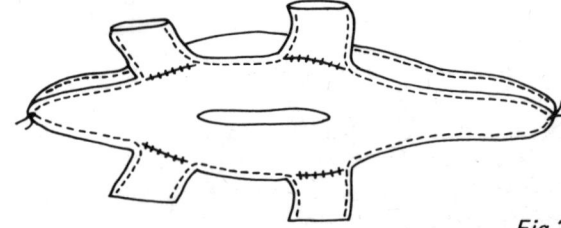

Fig 3

22

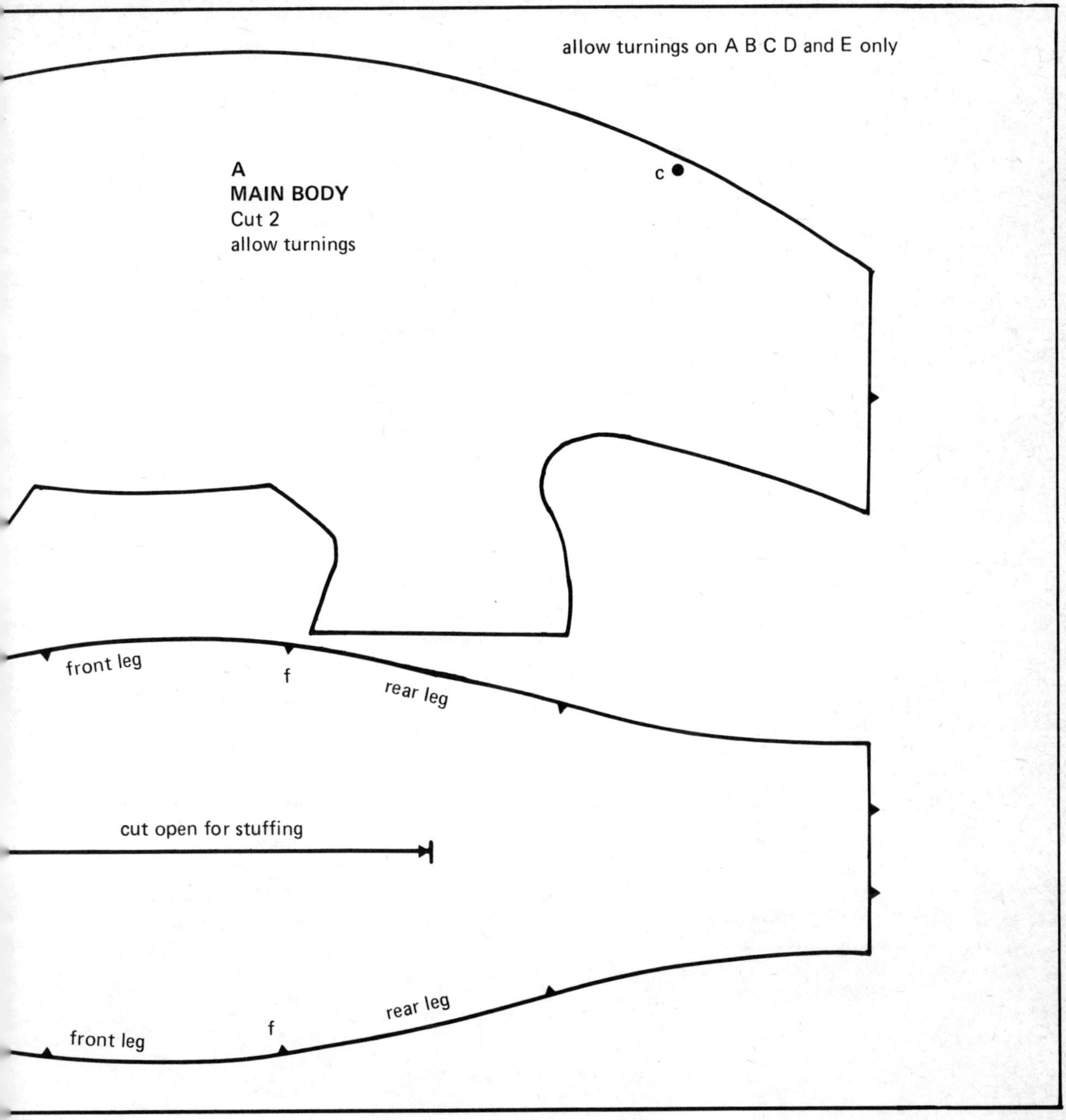

allow turnings on A B C D and E only

A
MAIN BODY
Cut 2
allow turnings

c ●

front leg

f

rear leg

cut open for stuffing

rear leg

front leg

f

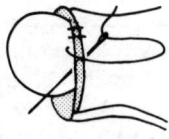

Fig 4

*Carefully trim away felt on roughly cut side (Fig. 7).

*Prepare wires by cutting to size —measure against each rib in turn and allow an extra $1\frac{1}{4}$in (3cm) on each wire. Bend over a small length at the top end of each wire and a larger loop at the other end (Fig. 8).

*Push each wire carefully into a rib on the sail (Fig. 6).

Setting the sail

*Pin the completed sail into the Dimetrodon's back opening and hand stab-stitch into place on right side of fabric, taking care to stitch securely around each wire (Fig. 9).

23

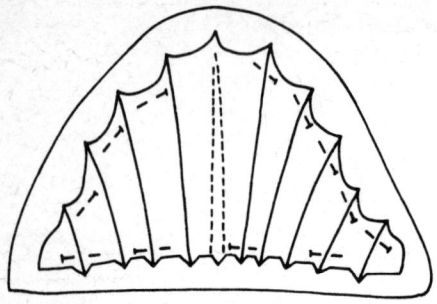

Fig 5

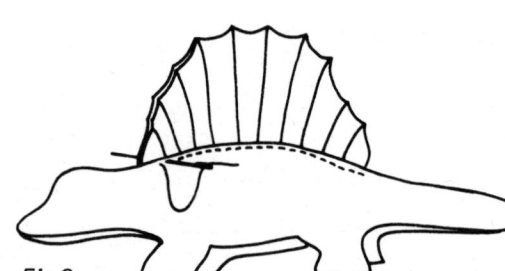

Fig 8

Fig 9

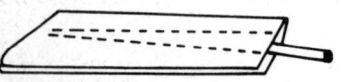

Fig 6

Fig 10

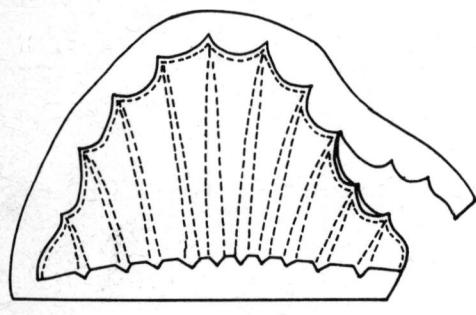

Fig 7

Fig 11

Stuffing

*Fill the Dimetrodon with stuffing. Begin with the head and tail, fill the body moulding the stuffing into the back, and placing it equally either side of the sail wires to ensure that the sail stands upright. Fill the legs and close the gap in the under-body and brush away the extra stuffing.

Feet

*Match and stitch together two foot shapes for each foot, three toes for front feet and five toes for rear feet. Slip-stitch completed feet to ends of legs (Fig. 10).

Features

If plastic eyes have not been used then cut out a circle of white felt and a tiny triangle of black felt. Pin the eye backings in place on the head and with a few stitches through the head secure the eyes and backings. The eye lids are

1 *Left to right:* The Armour-Plated Lizard (*Stegosaurus*); Three-Horned Dinosaur (*Triceratops*); Loch Ness Monster (*Plesiosaur*) and a Woolly Mammoth.

2   *Below, left to right:* Woolly Mammoth, 2 contrasting Sail-Back
Lizards (*Dimetrodon*) and hovering above, a Lizard-Bird
(*Pteranodon*).

3   Kings of the Monsters: *Left:* Spike-Thumbed Dinosaur
(*Iguanodon*); *right:* Tyrannosaurus.

4   *Bottom:* Fish-Lizard (*Ichthyosaur*); *left:* Thunder-Lizard (*Brontosaurus*); *right:* Stegosaurus; *top:* Mammoth.

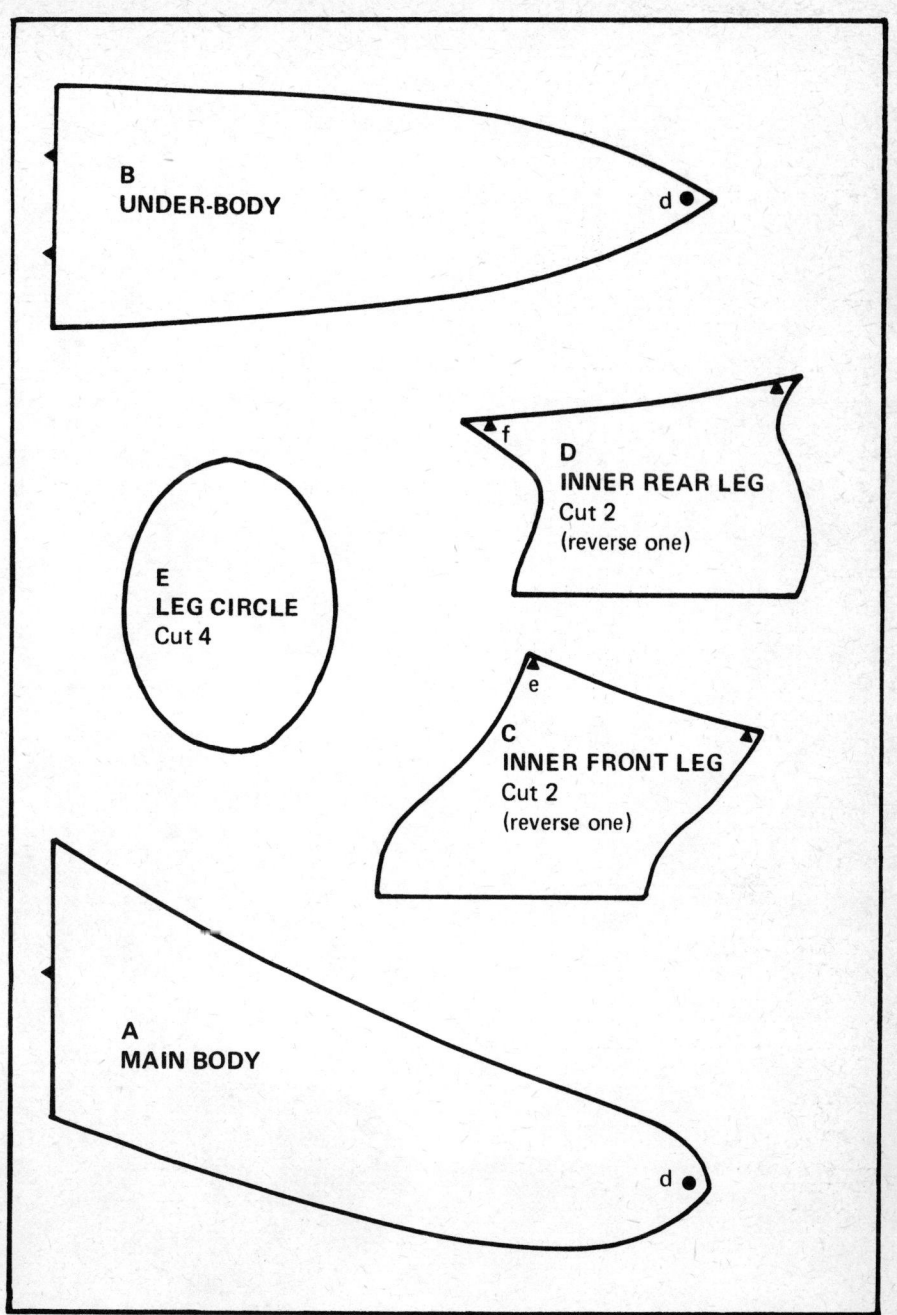

B
UNDER-BODY

d ●

f
D
INNER REAR LEG
Cut 2
(reverse one)

E
LEG CIRCLE
Cut 4

e
C
INNER FRONT LEG
Cut 2
(reverse one)

A
MAIN BODY

d ●

stitched over the eyes which give a lizard-like effect. Embroider the mouth and nostrils in stem stitch using black thread. A row of white stitches can indicate teeth (Fig. 11).

Ichthyosaur: Fish-Lizard

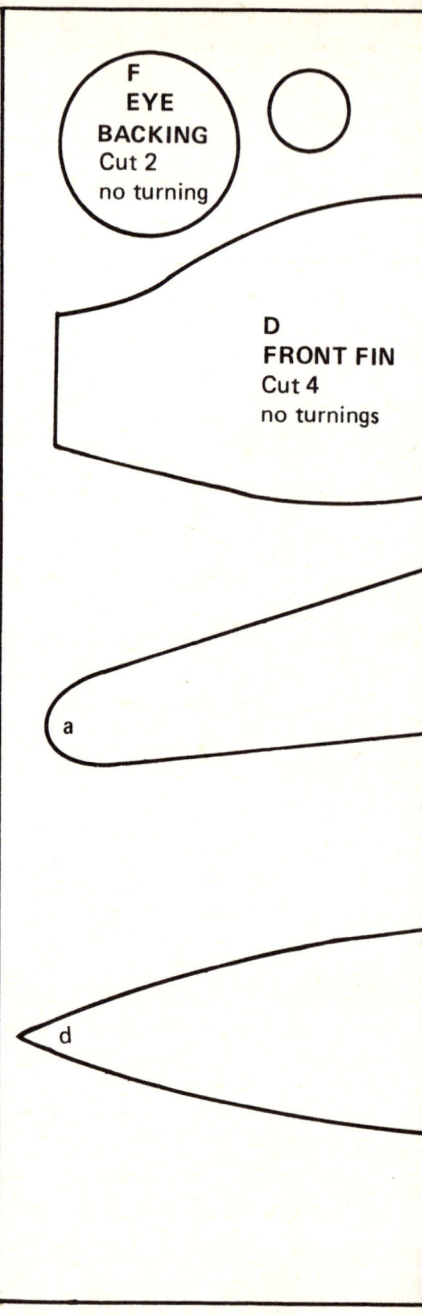

Ichthyosaur (fish-lizard) was a swimming reptile that lived in America and Europe during the Jurassic Period, 150 million years ago. It looked just like the modern dolphin but, being a reptile, was cold-blooded, though it is thought to have given birth to live young instead of laying eggs. Icthyosaurs grew to about ten feet (3m) long, though many were much smaller. The first one was discovered by Mary Anning, a young girl, in Lyme Regis, Dorset, England, about 150 years ago. The ichthyosaur, although it evolved from a four-footed land reptile, was perfectly adapted for life in the sea and swam with beats of its powerful tail. Its forelimbs were little paddles for steering, while its hind limbs had disappeared. It fed on fish and shell-fish.

MATERIALS REQUIRED

Main body fabric: 14 x 21ins (35 x 52cm)

Contrast felt: 14 x 10ins (35 x 25 cm)

Plastic safety eyes 12mm (optional) or scraps of black and white felt

Embroidery thread

Sewing cotton

Card for stiffening tail (optional)

Stuffing: 8oz (226g)

Size of Model: Length 21ins (52 cm); Girth 9ins (22cm)

MAKING-UP

Patterns

Make up patterns as explained in Hints and Instructions. Pieces required are: 2 main bodies (A);

1 under-body (B); 2 upper fin (C); 4 front fins (D); 4 rear fins (E); 2 eye backings (F).

Cutting out

Place patterns pieces on the fabrics, main bodies and under-body on main fabric. All the fins and the eye backing on the contrast felt. (Note: if using brushed nylon it is effective to use the smooth side for the main body and the brushed side for the under-body). Mark round the patterns and cut out, remembering to allow turnings as explained in Hints and Instructions.

Sewing

Fins

*Match together both sections of the upper fin and top stitch round the edges, leaving open the lower side (Fig. 1). A piece of card cut to the shape shown as a guide on the pattern can be inserted as an optional stiffening. Stitch together two front fin shapes and also two rear fin shapes and repeat

28

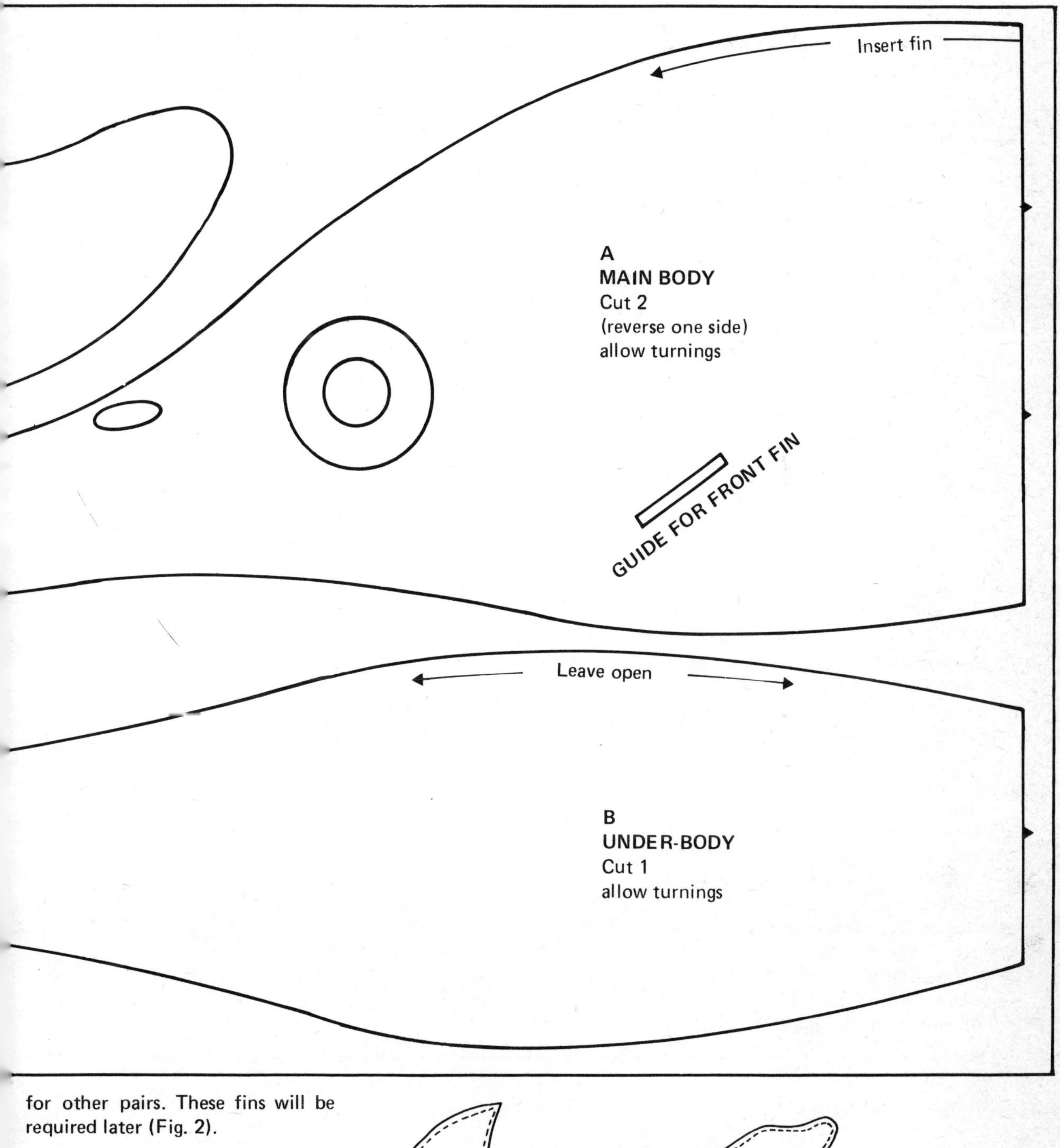

Insert fin

A
MAIN BODY
Cut 2
(reverse one side)
allow turnings

GUIDE FOR FRONT FIN

Leave open

B
UNDER-BODY
Cut 1
allow turnings

for other pairs. These fins will be
required later (Fig. 2).

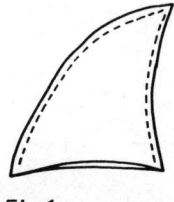

Fig 1

Fig 2

Body

*Stay stitch around curves of tail (Fig. 3).

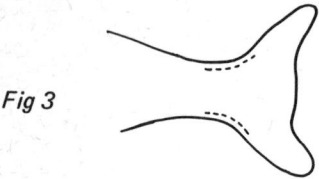

Fig 3

*Pin upper fin to right side of main body section. Baste in place (Fig. 4).

*Right sides together lay other main body over fin and body.

*Pin and stitch all round from 'a' at mouth, along back, around tail 'b' to 'c' at end of tail fin (Fig. 5).

*If plastic eyes are to be used turn head to right side, pin eye backing in place and fix eye following Hints and Instructions.

Under-body

*Right sides together, (Note: This could mean opposite side of brushed nylon, see note above) pin and stitch under-body to the main body on one side securing stitches at both ends. Repeat for other side, leaving opening for stuffing (Fig. 6).

*Stitch together seam from the end of the under-body to the end of the tail fin 'c'.

*Trim seam and clip to curves.

*Turn Ichthyosaur to right side, easing out nose and tail fin with the stuffing stick.

*Optional tail stiffening. Cut a piece of card shaped as on pattern guide and insert this into tail.

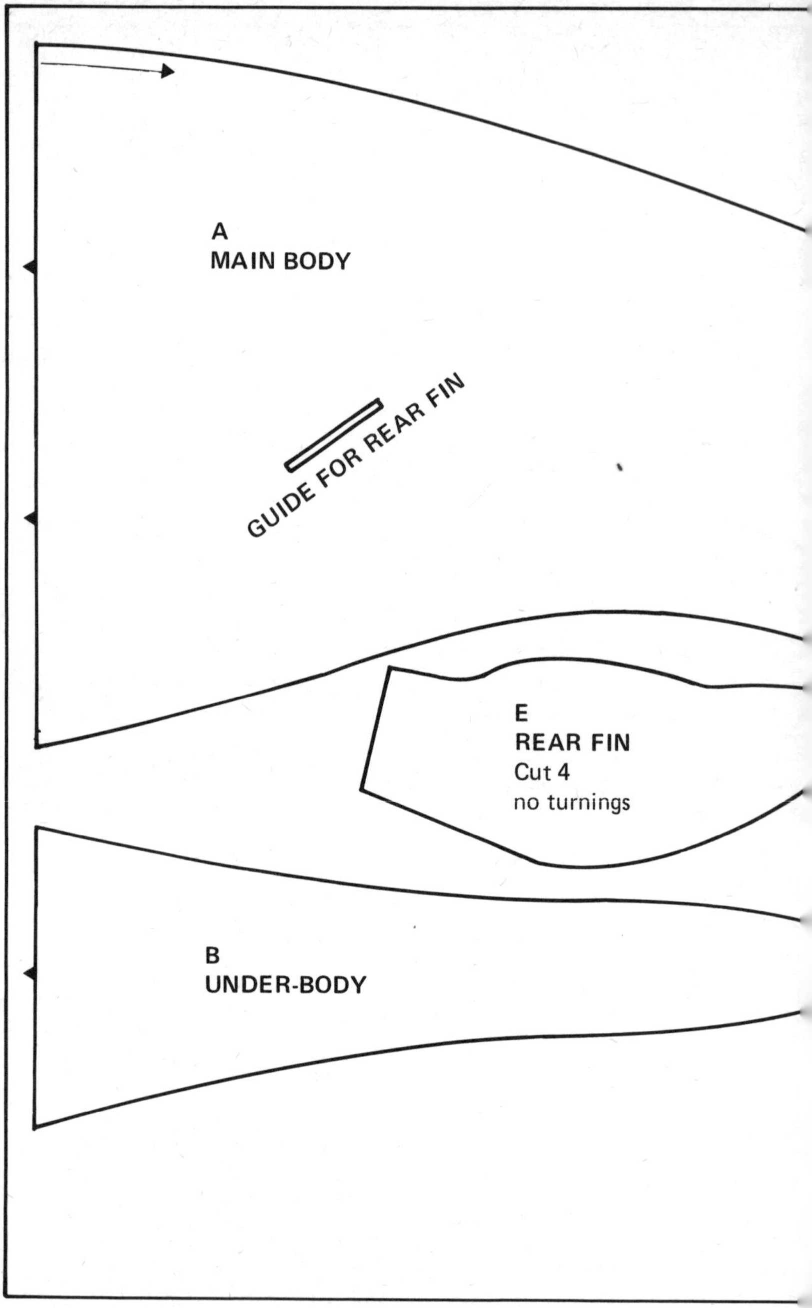

A
MAIN BODY

GUIDE FOR REAR FIN

E
REAR FIN
Cut 4
no turnings

B
UNDER-BODY

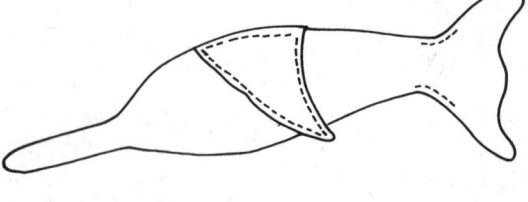

Fig 4

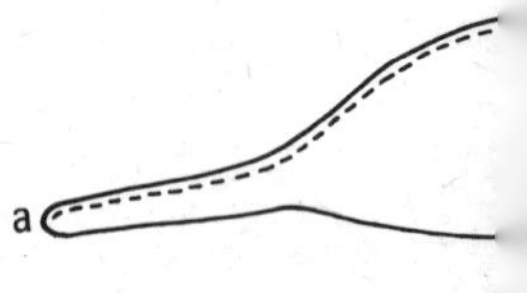

a

Fig 5

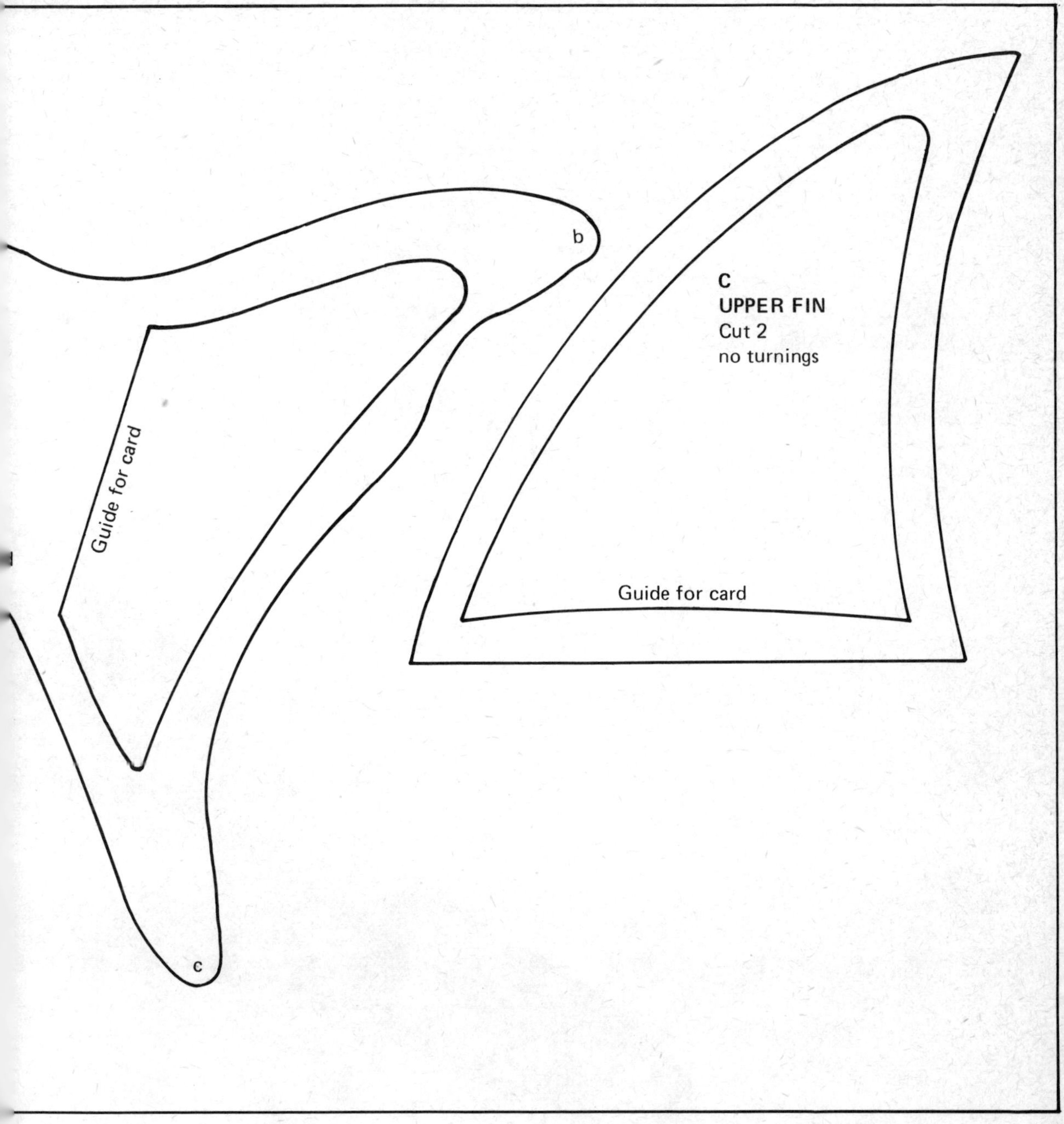

b

C
UPPER FIN
Cut 2
no turnings

Guide for card

Guide for card

c

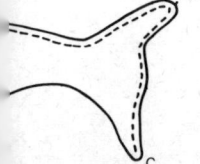

b

c

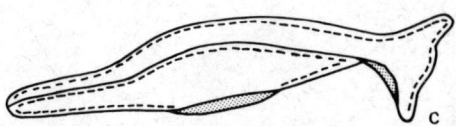

c

Fig 6

*Make a line of hand stitching to separate the tail from the body (Fig. 7).

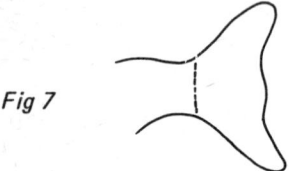

Fig 7

*Fill the creature with stuffing, easing small quantities into the nose with the stuffing stick and gradually filling the body, close the gap and brush to remove excess filling.

*Pin the fins onto the body along the guide lines and stitch in position (Fig. 8).

Finishing

*If plastic eyes have not been used cut two small back eye dots and two larger white circles. Stitch these on to the eye backing and slip stitch the eye to the head.

*Work a line of stem stitch to indicate the mouth. A few stitches are made through the head to shape the nostrils which are marked with satin stitches (Fig. 9).

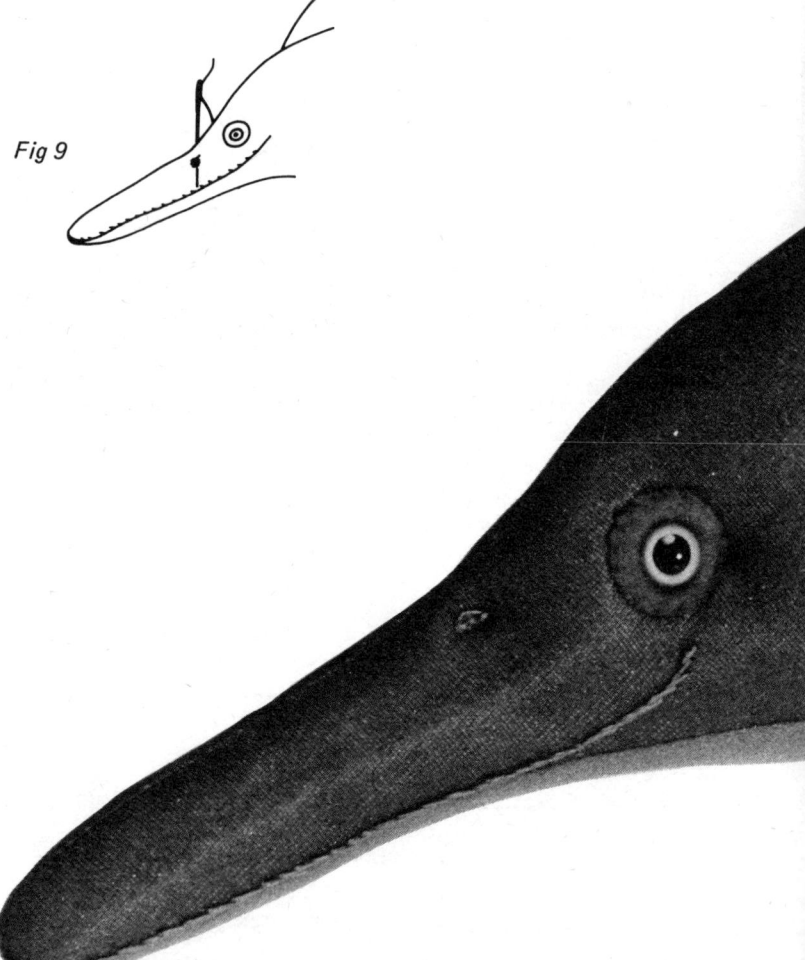

Fig 9

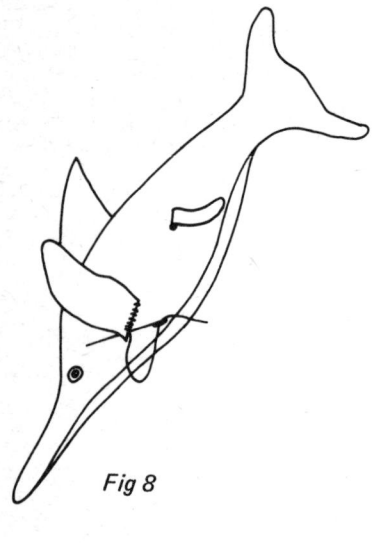

Fig 8

Iguanodon: The Spike-Thumb Dinosaur

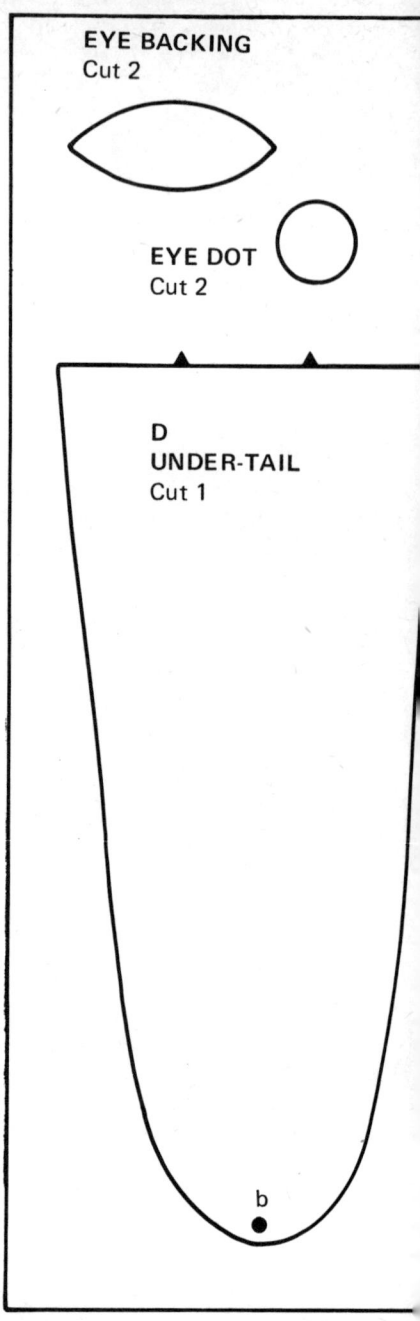

EYE BACKING
Cut 2

EYE DOT
Cut 2

D
UNDER-TAIL
Cut 1

b

Iguanodon (iguana-teeth) was a large plant-eating dinosaur which lived at the beginning of the Cretaceous Period, 125 million years ago. Bones and teeth of this animal are not too uncommon in the Cretaceous rocks of southern England, where a great river delta was in existence. The fossilized remains of a complete herd of Iguanodon were found in Belgium and are now on show in the museum in Brussels. A full-grown Iguanodon stood 15 feet (4.5 m) tall and was 30 feet (9 m) from head to tail. It had special-ized teeth for crushing and eating the leaves of the ferns and small trees that lived at the time. Its only defence against hungry meat-eaters seems to have been a strong bony spike on its hand, for in spite of its powerful hind legs, Iguanodon was too large and heavy to be able to run very fast.

MATERIALS REQUIRED

Main body of fabric or felt (orange):
  18 x 36ins (45 x 90 cm)
Contrast felt: 10 x 10in (25 x 25 cm)
Plastic safety eyes (8 or 10mm) or scraps of black and white felt
Thin black wool or embroidery thread
Sewing cotton
Stuffing: 8oz (226g)
Oddments of wool or coloured felts for scarf
Size of model: Length 10ins (25 cm); Height 14ins (35 cm)
Note: This model is rather smaller than it should be compared to the other designs. However it is much easier to make at this scale.

MAKING-UP

Patterns

Make up patterns as explained in Hints and Instructions. Pattern shapes required are: 2 main bodies (A); 1 centre body gusset (B); 2 inner legs (C); 1 under-tail (D); 2 leg circles (E); 4 hands (F); 4 feet (G); 2 eye backings (H).

Cutting-out

Lay pattern pieces on to fabrics: 2 main bodies; 1 centre body gusset; 2 inner legs; 1 under-tail, 2 leg circles on main colour (orange). 4 hands; 4 feet and 2 eye backings on the contrast felt. Cut out following Hints and Instructions.

Sewing

*Stay-stitch under chin on both main body shapes (Fig. 1), and around angle of arms (Fig. 2).
*With right sides together pin and stitch both main body shapes together from 'a' at mouth around head and back to 'b' at end of tail (Fig. 3).

34

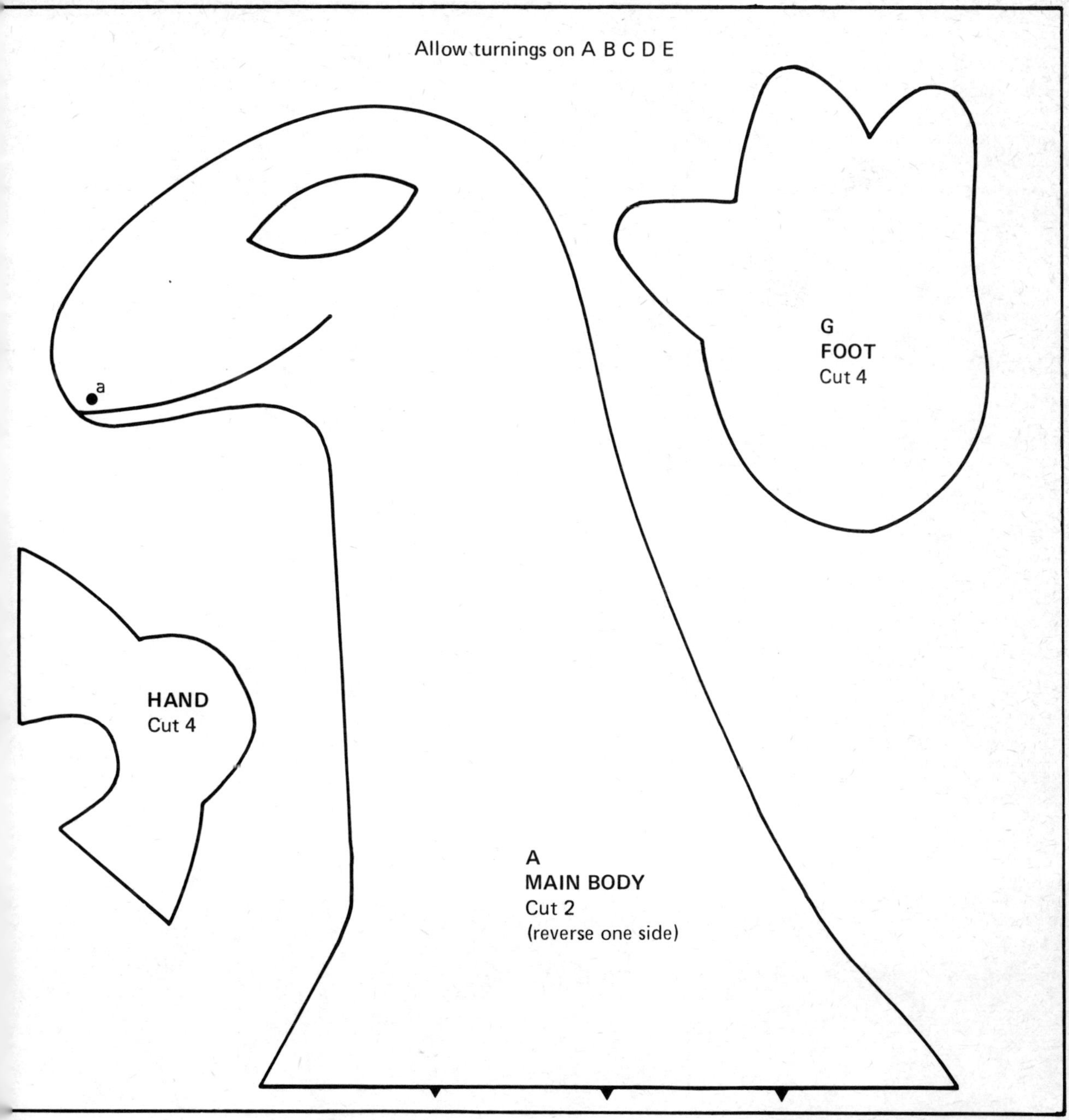

Allow turnings on A B C D E

**G
FOOT
Cut 4**

a

**HAND
Cut 4**

**A
MAIN BODY
Cut 2
(reverse one side)**

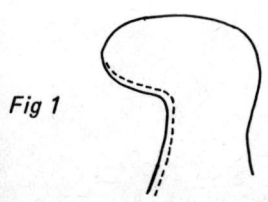

Fig 1

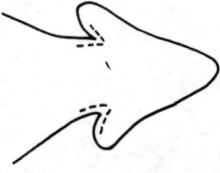

Fig 2

*If plastic eyes are used, turn head to right side, smooth out centre seam and fix eyes with the backings following Hints and In-structions.

*With right sides together pin and stitch both inner legs to the centre front gusset matching 'c' and 'd' (Fig. 4).

*With right sides together pin completed centre gusset to main bodies, matching 'a' at mouth and continuing to 'e'. Ease to fit and clip to stay stitching if necessary. Stitch all round edge of gusset including arms but leaving open the ends of the legs and the side seam from 'e' to 'f' (Fig. 5).

*Pin under-tail to main bodies, matching 'f' 'g' and 'b'. Stitch, leaving open 'f' to 'g' on both sides as a gap for turning and stuffing (Fig. 6).

*Fit a leg circle into the ends of the legs and oversew as explained in Hints and Instructions.

*Check that no pins remain in the fabric. Turn Iguanodon to right side out, easing out the arms and tail with the stuffing stick.

Stuffing

*Fill with stuffing, working with only small amounts at a time and placing it in position in the head and arms and tail with the blunt stick. Iguanodon will balance and stand perfectly if the legs and tail are firmly filled. Pin together the gap under the tail and oversew. Take out the pins and brush to remove excess stuffing.

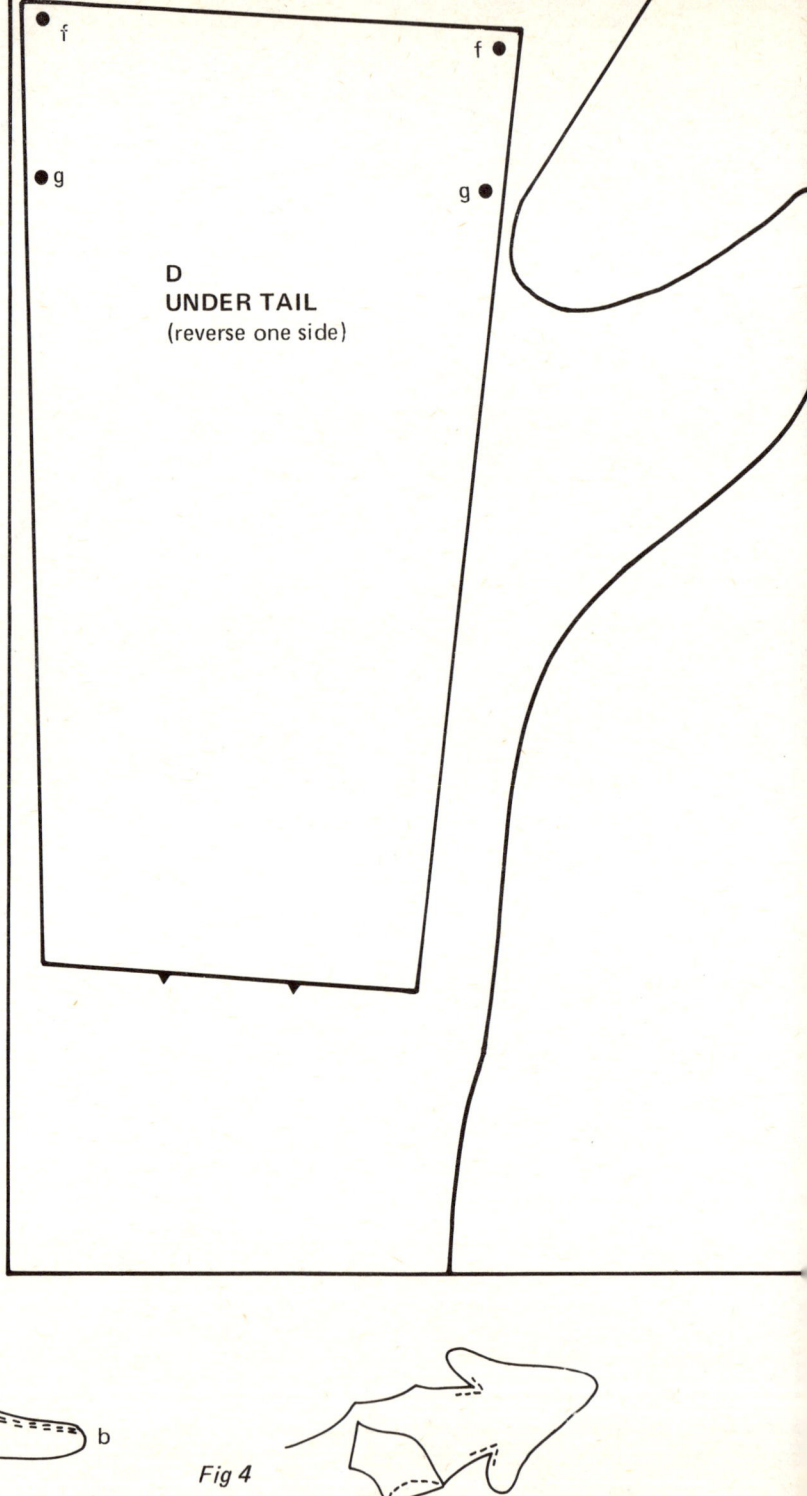

D
UNDER TAIL
(reverse one side)

Fig 3

Fig 4

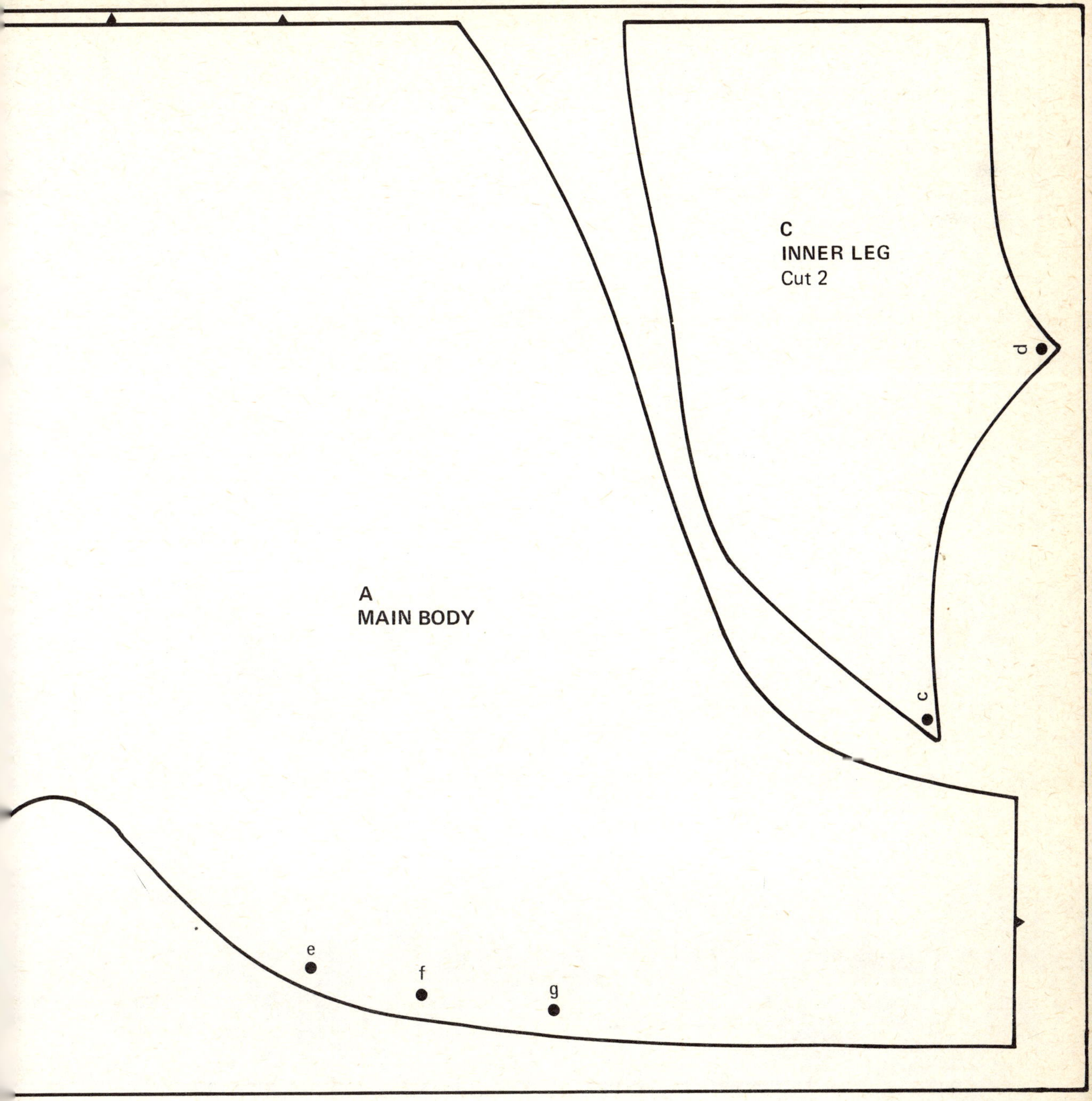

C
INNER LEG
Cut 2

d •

c
•

A
MAIN BODY

e
•

f
•

g
•

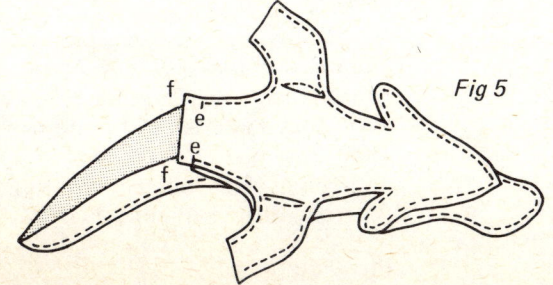

f
e
e
f

Fig 5

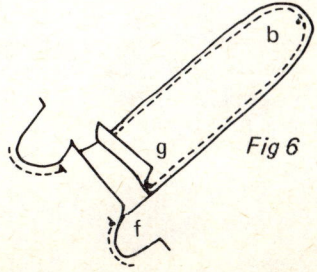

b

g

Fig 6

f

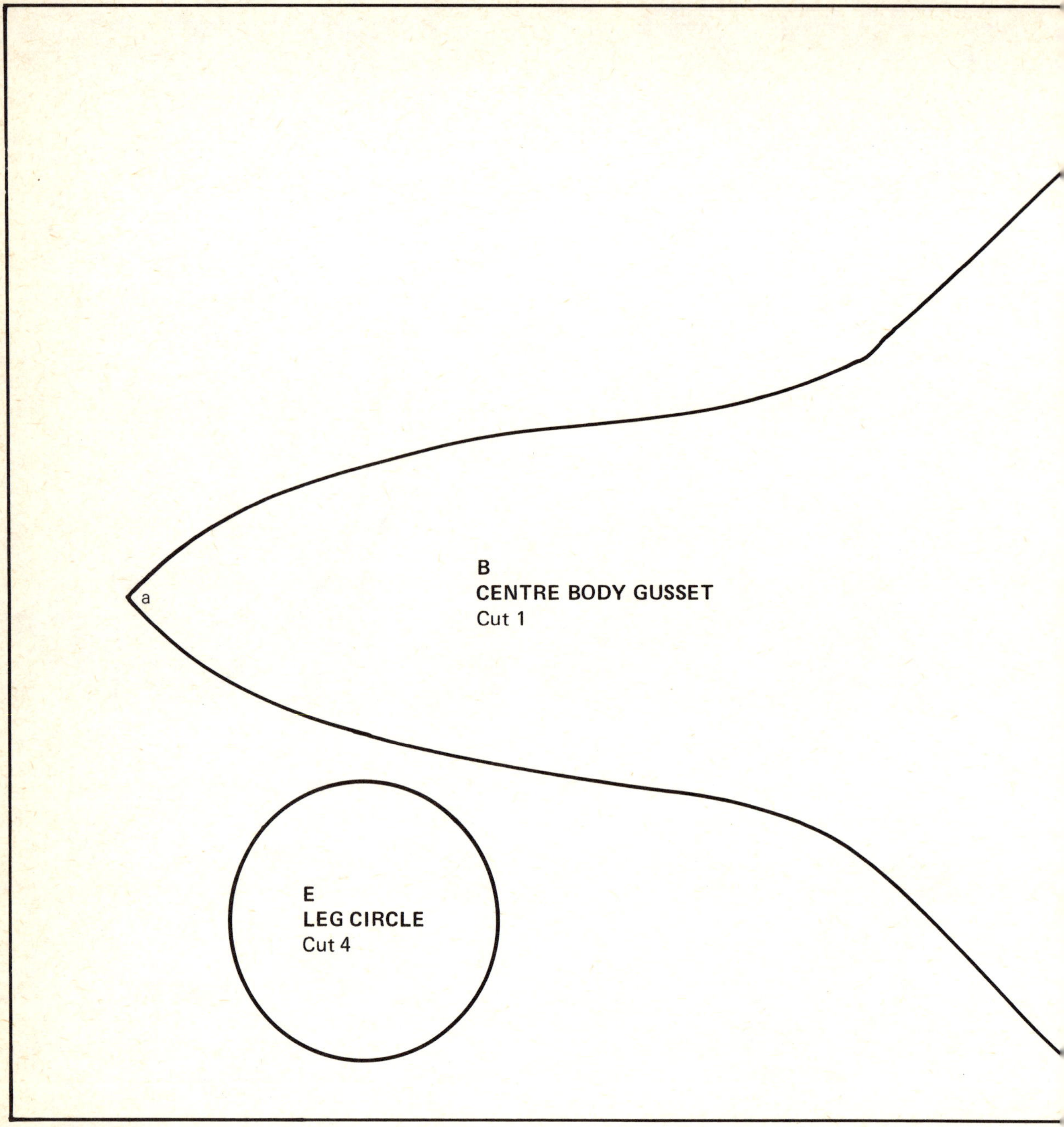

B
CENTRE BODY GUSSET
Cut 1

a

E
LEG CIRCLE
Cut 4

Hands

*Match together two hand shapes and top stitch them (Fig. 7). Sew to the ends of the arms, the larger thumb upwards (Fig. 8).

Fig 7

Feet

*Match and stitch together two foot shapes for each foot. Make a small cross in the top fabric only of each foot and insert a little stuffing (Fig. 9).

*Stitch feet to ends of legs, covering the open slits (Fig. 10).

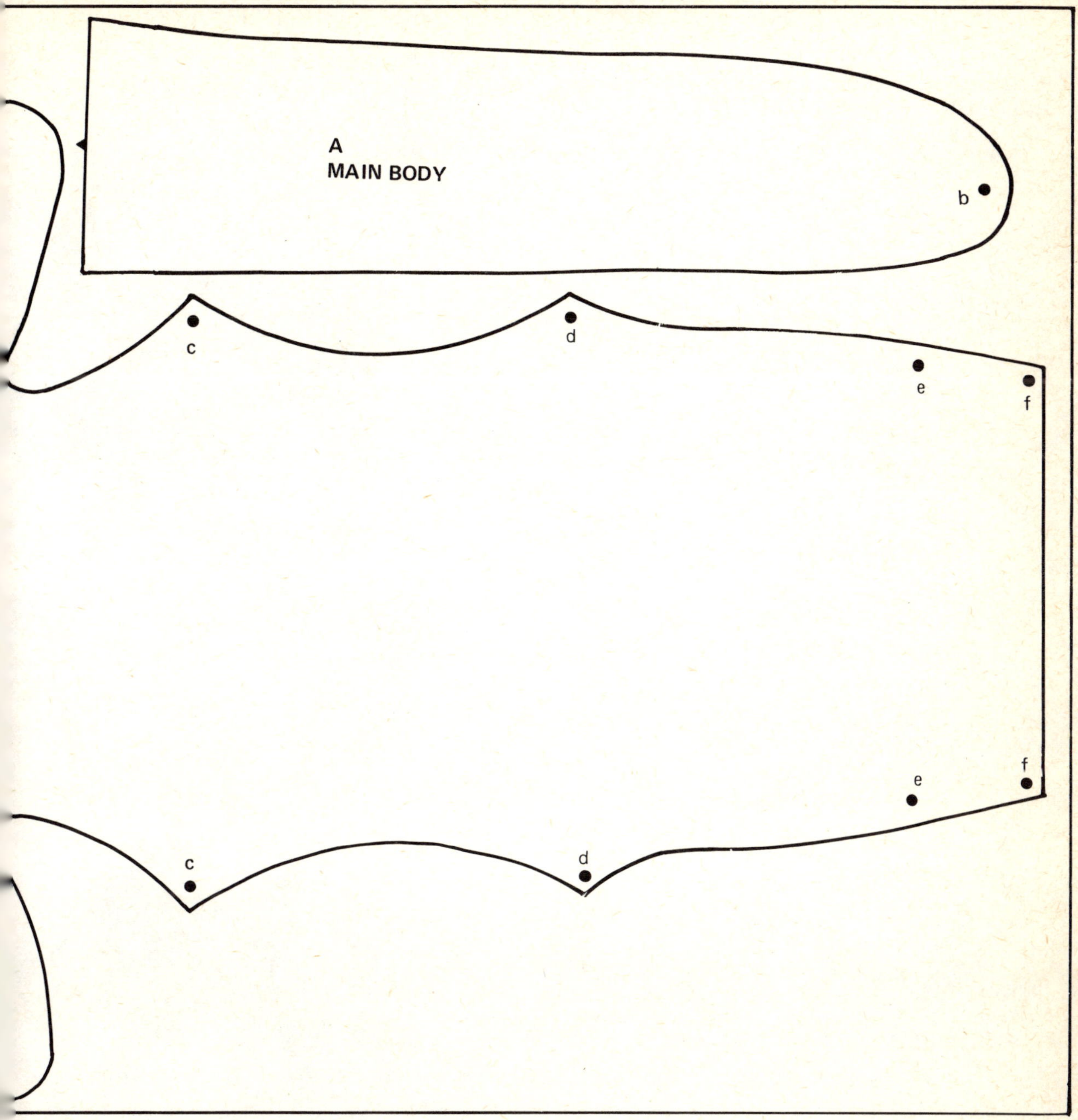

A
MAIN BODY

b •

• c

• d

• e

• f

• e

• f

• c

• d

• e

• f

Fig 8

Fig 9

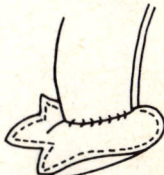

Fig 10

Features

*Work a line of stem stitch to make the smiling mouth and mark each nostril with a few stitches (Fig. 11).

Fig 11

Scarf

*A scarf can be made from rectangles of felt 1½ins (4 cm) by 2½ins (6.5cm) stitched together on the shorter edges and the end fringed, or a scarf can be knitted with oddments of coloured 4-ply wool. Cast on 10 stitches with No. 9 or 10 knitting needles, knit in garter stitch for as long as required or as much wool as you have. The scarf illustrated is approximately 30ins (76cm) long. The ends can have a knotted fringe. Note that each time a different colour is used, sufficient wool must be left of both colours to darn in to the scarf to secure.

*Press finished scarf.

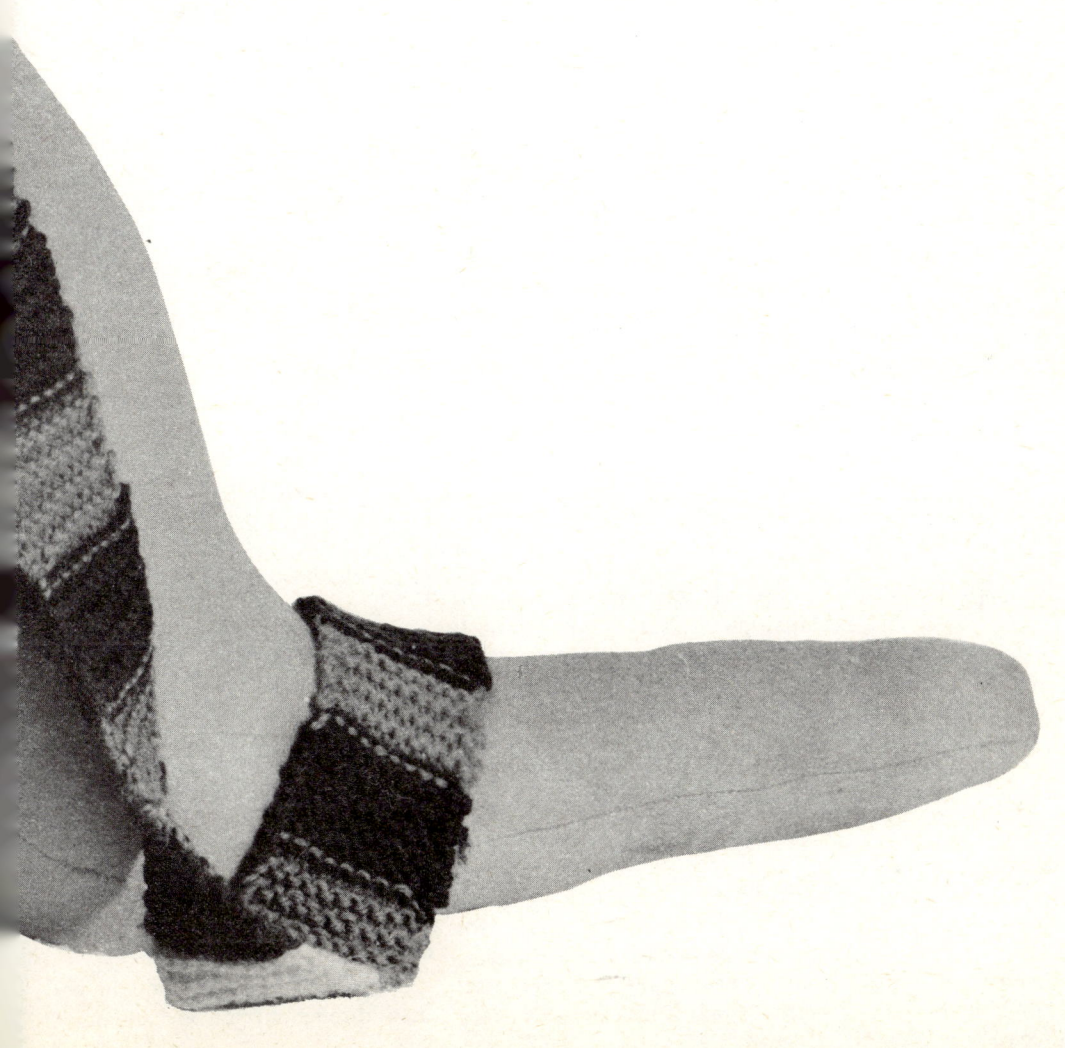

Woolly Mammoth

The Woolly Mammoth, Mammuthus primigenius, lived in the frozen tundra of Europe and North America at the time of the Ice Age. It was a little smaller than the modern Indian elephant but had much longer curved tusks that sometimes crossed over in old males. The mammoth was covered with a thick coat of coarse reddish brown fur. His bones and teeth are often found in gravel pits in the south of England, while in Siberia complete bodies have been found, preserved for thousands of years in a natural 'deep freeze'. In addition, paintings and carvings of the mammoth done by prehistoric man are preserved in caves in France and elsewhere. All in all we have a good idea what the woolly mammoth looked like even though the last one must have died about 10,000 years ago.

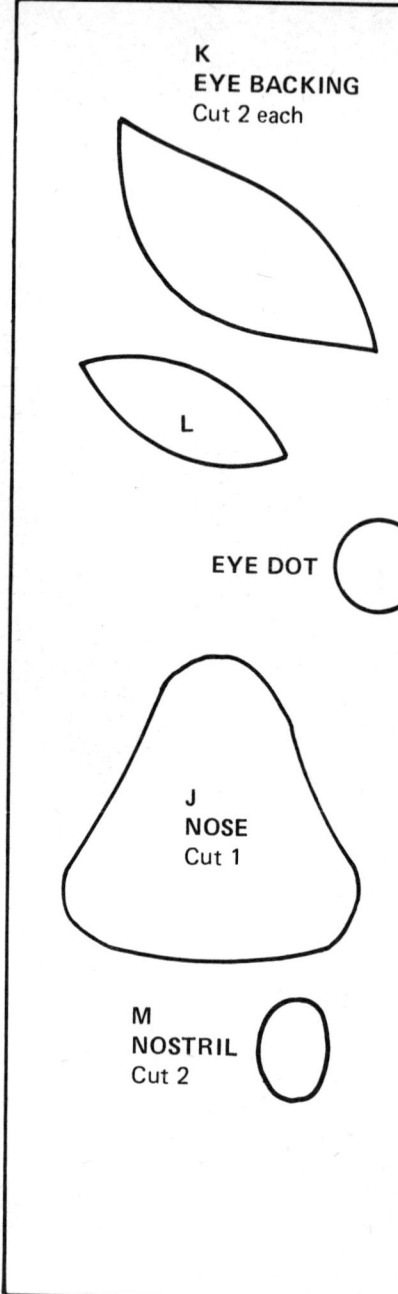

**K
EYE BACKING**
Cut 2 each

L

EYE DOT

**J
NOSE**
Cut 1

**M
NOSTRIL**
Cut 2

MATERIALS REQUIRED

Fur fabric: 55 x 28ins (137 x 70 cm)

Dark felt for feet: 12 x 12ins (30 x 30cm)

Light felt for nose and eye backing: 6 x 6ins (15 x 15cm)

White or light felt for tusks: 12 x 14ins (30 x 35cm)

Plastic safety eyes (optional): 12mm

2 lengths of wire (optional): each 18ins (45cm)

Card for foot discs

Sewing cotton

Strong thread

Stuffing: 2lbs (1kg)

Size of Model: Length 18ins (45 cm);

Height 12ins (30cm)

MAKING-UP

Patterns

Make up patterns as explained in Hints and Instructions. Pattern shapes required are: 2 main body (A); 2 under-bodies (B); 1 centre head gusset (C); 1 back gusset (D); 4 ears (E); 1 tail (F); 2 tusk pockets (G); 4 leg circles (H); 4 tusks (I); 1 nose (J); 2 eye backings (K); 2 eye backings (L); 2 nostrils (M).

Cutting-out

Place pattern pieces on the fabrics: 2 main bodies; 2 under-bodies; 1 centre head gusset; 1 back gusset; 4 ears; 1 tail; 2 tusk pockets on to fur fabric. Four leg circles; 2 eye backings; 2 nostrils on to dark felt. One nose and 2 eye backings on to light felt. Four tusks on to white or light felt.

Sewing

Note: Strong thread should be used throughout for all hand sewings.

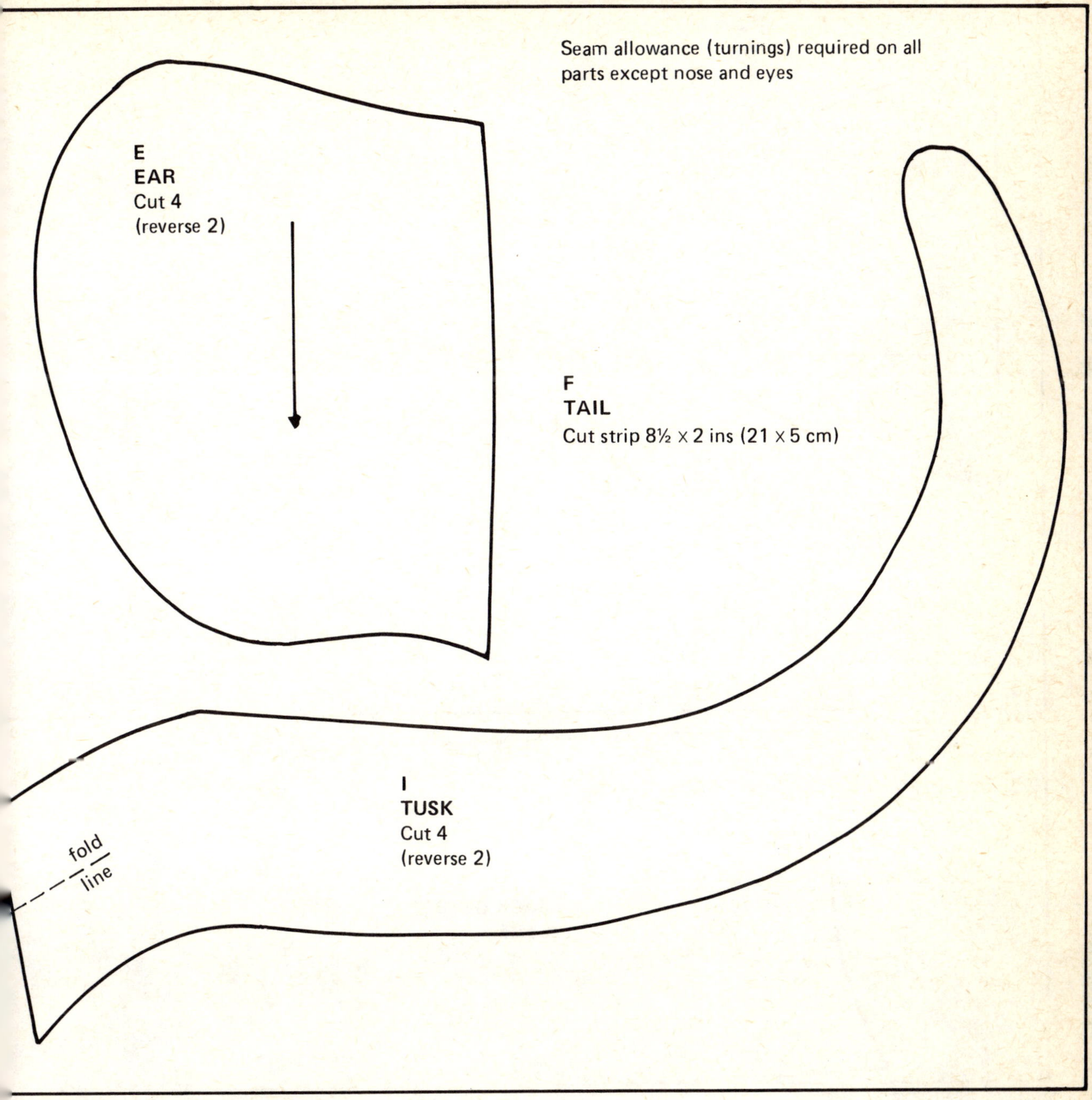

Seam allowance (turnings) required on all parts except nose and eyes

E
EAR
Cut 4
(reverse 2)

F
TAIL
Cut strip 8½ × 2 ins (21 × 5 cm)

I
TUSK
Cut 4
(reverse 2)

fold
line

*Stay stitch to reinforce the head around hump on both sections (Fig. 1).

*With right sides together join centre head gusset (C) to back gusset (D) matching 'e' and 'f'. Trim seam (Fig. 2).

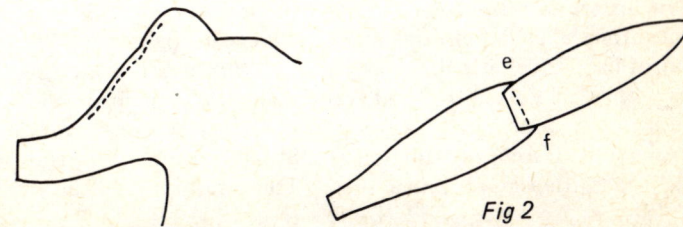

Fig 1

e

f

Fig 2

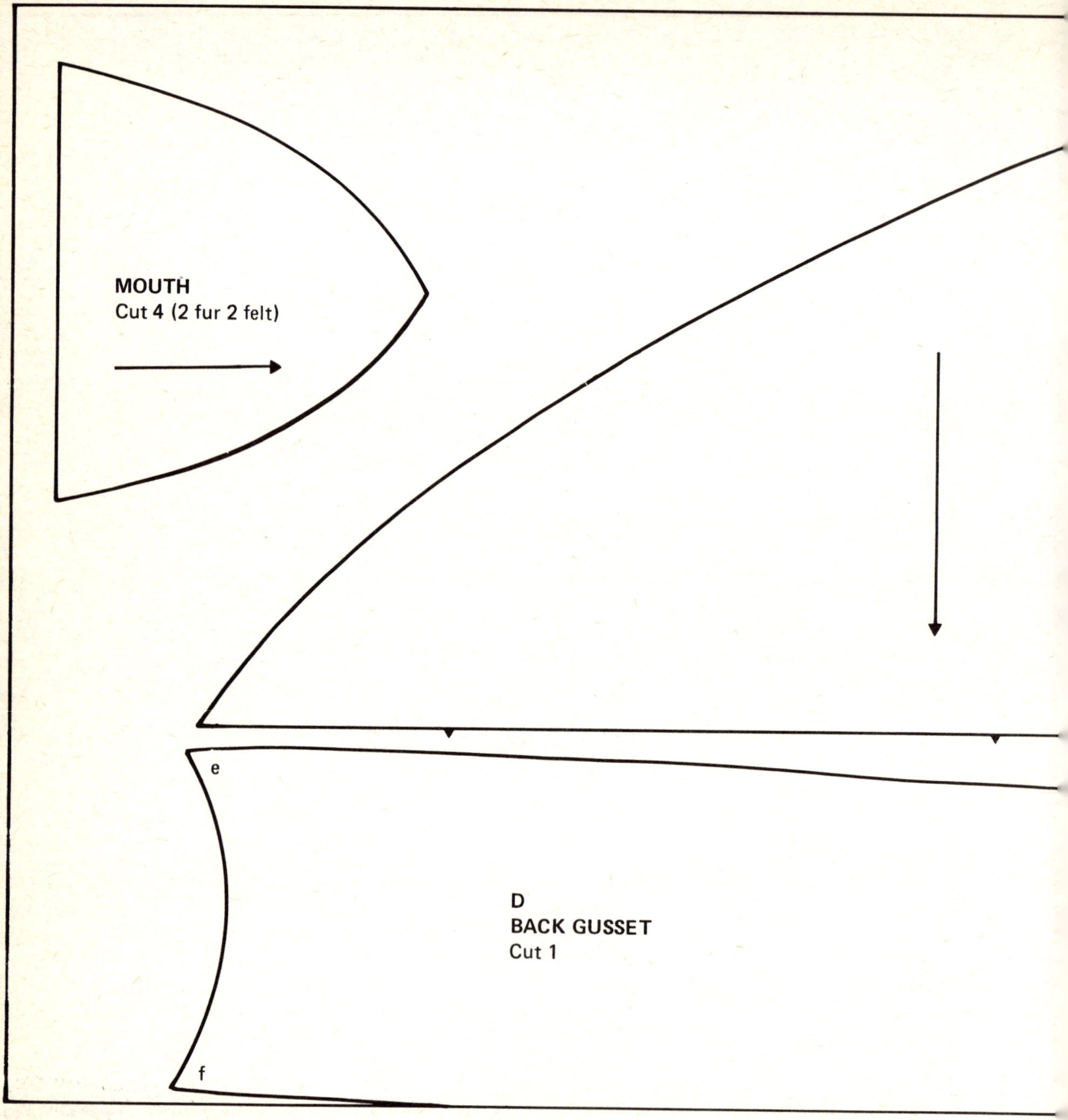

MOUTH
Cut 4 (2 fur 2 felt)

e

D
BACK GUSSET
Cut 1

f

*Right sides together pin complete gusset to main body by sections from 'a' at end of trunk along top of back to 'c' at tail, matching seam at 'b'. Ease side of head and trunk to fit. Stitch from 'a' to 'c' breaking and securing stitches at both ends. Repeat for other side.

*Stitch leg arcs on wrong (woven) side of under-bodies by folding leg on line and stitching along curved line (Fig. 3).

*With right sides together pin under-body to main body section, matching 'c' rear and 'd' front. Stitch leaving open ends of legs. Trim seam and clip to curves (Fig. 4).

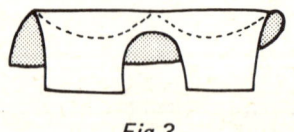

Fig 3

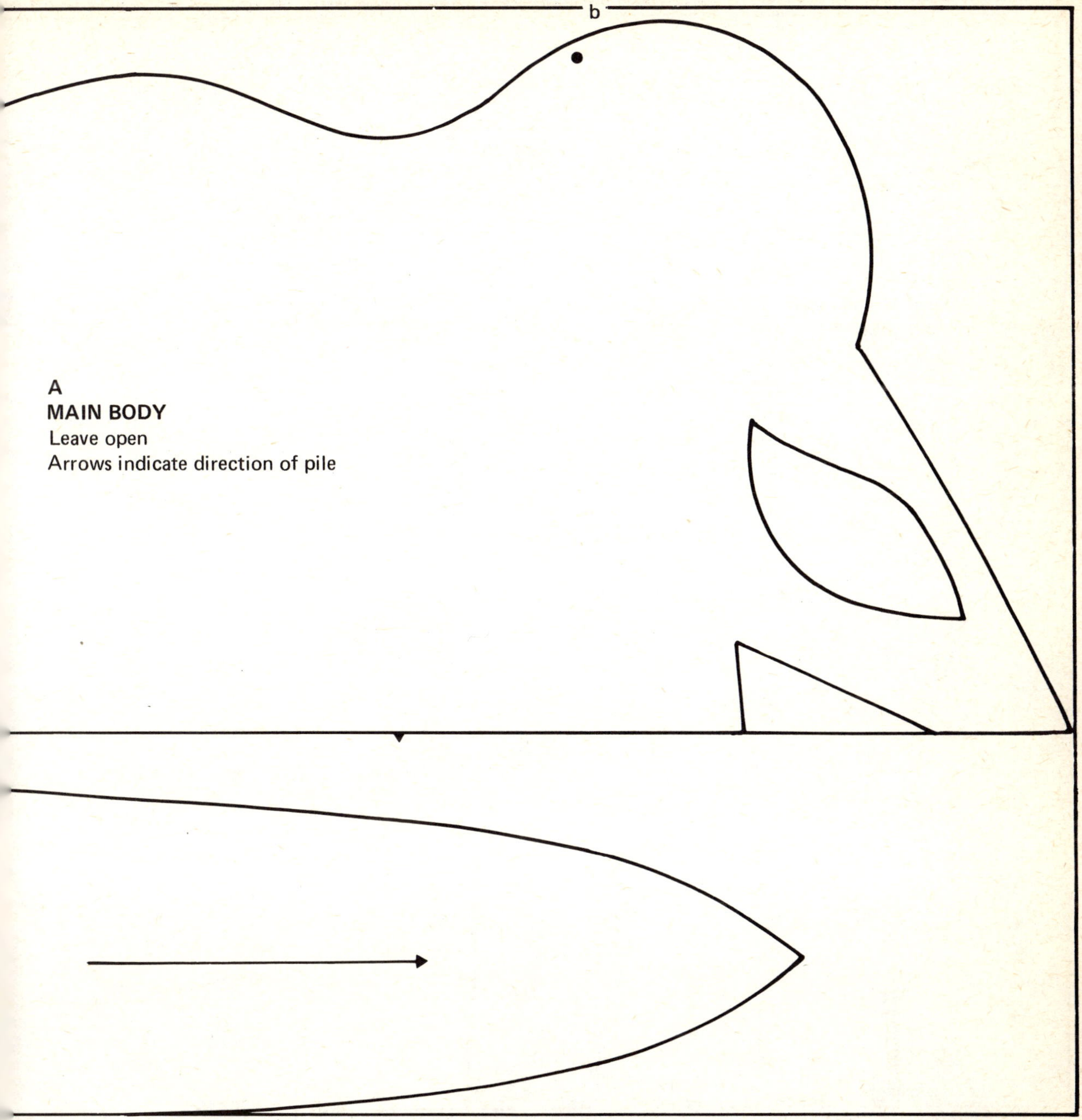

b

A
MAIN BODY
Leave open
Arrows indicate direction of pile

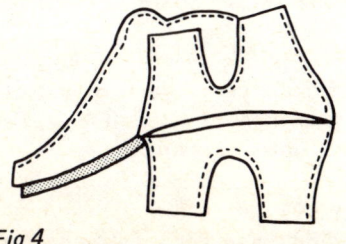

Fig 4

*Pin together centre seam of trunk and under-bodies. Stitch leaving open gap for stuffing and breaking stitching at join of under-bodies.

*Insert foot circle into end of leg. Smooth pile of fur and hand back stitch in place. Repeat for other legs (Fig. 5).

*Check that no pins remain in the fabric. Turn Mammoth to right side, easing out the trunk with the stuffing stick.

*Turn in the edge at the end of the trunk and pin nose in position, stitch securely (Fig. 6). Cut four small discs of cardboard slightly

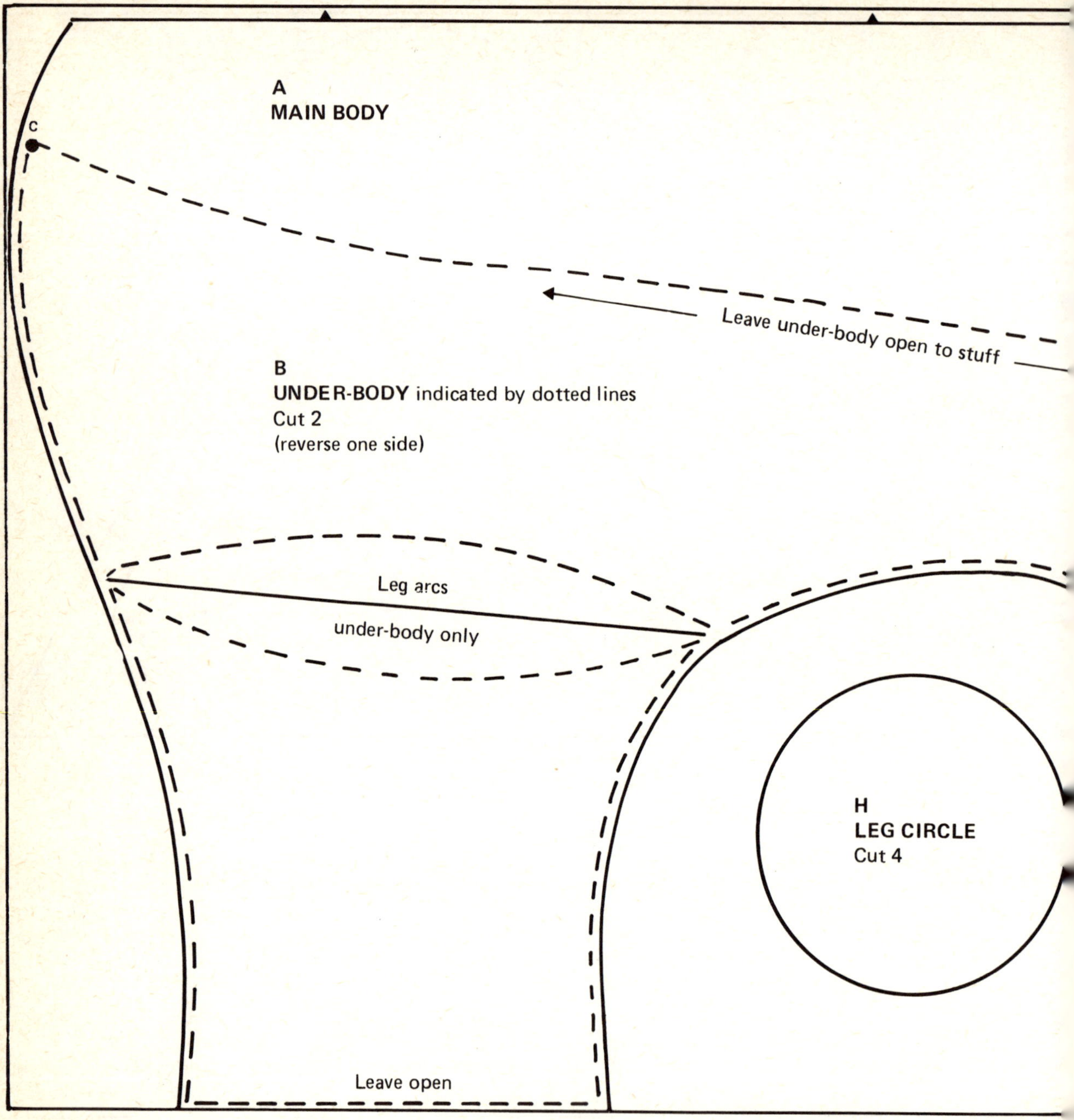

c

A
MAIN BODY

Leave under-body open to stuff →

B
UNDER-BODY indicated by dotted lines
Cut 2
(reverse one side)

Leg arcs

under-body only

H
LEG CIRCLE
Cut 4

Leave open

smaller than pattern (H) and put into ends of legs.

*If plastic eyes are to be used, position them on the two eye backings and fix in place. (Fig. 7) See also Hints and Instructions.

Stuffing

*Fill Mammoth following sug-

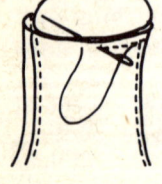

Fig 5

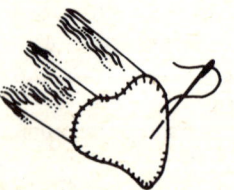

Fig 6

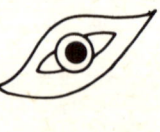

Fig 7

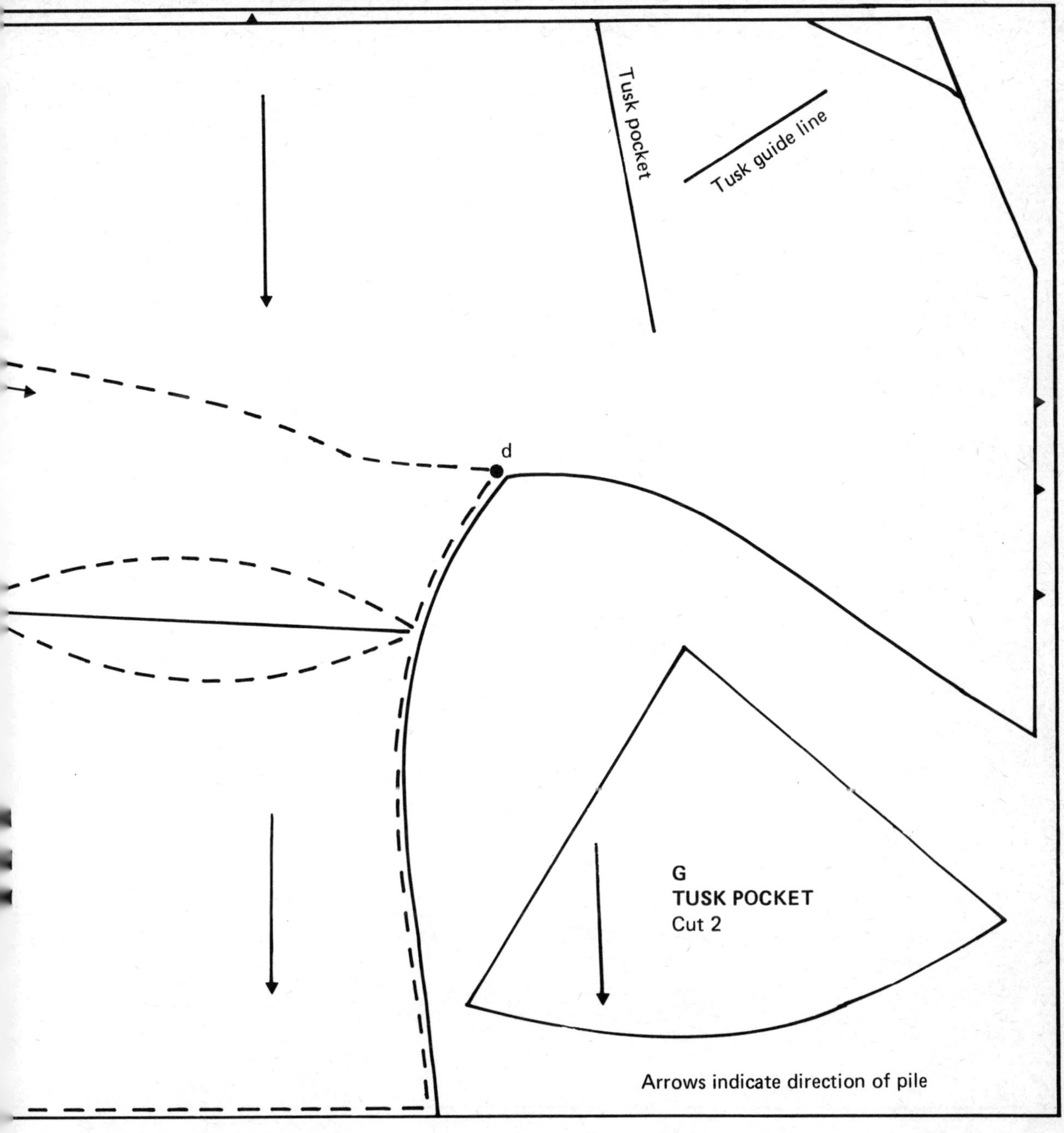

Tusk pocket

Tusk guide line

d

**G
TUSK POCKET
Cut 2**

Arrows indicate direction of pile

gestions in Hints and Instructions. Begin with the head, carefully moulding the trunk, jaw and hump. When the body is partly filled, two wires can be placed in the legs, the stuffing of the legs and body is then completed but the Mammoth will stand quite successfully if the legs are filled firmly. Close the gap and brush fur to remove excess filling.

Finishing

*Make a dart in the centre of one pair of ears (this can be omitted if long hair fur is used) to make inner ears (Fig. 8). With right sides together stitch one inner and one outer ear together leaving open the

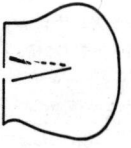

Fig 8

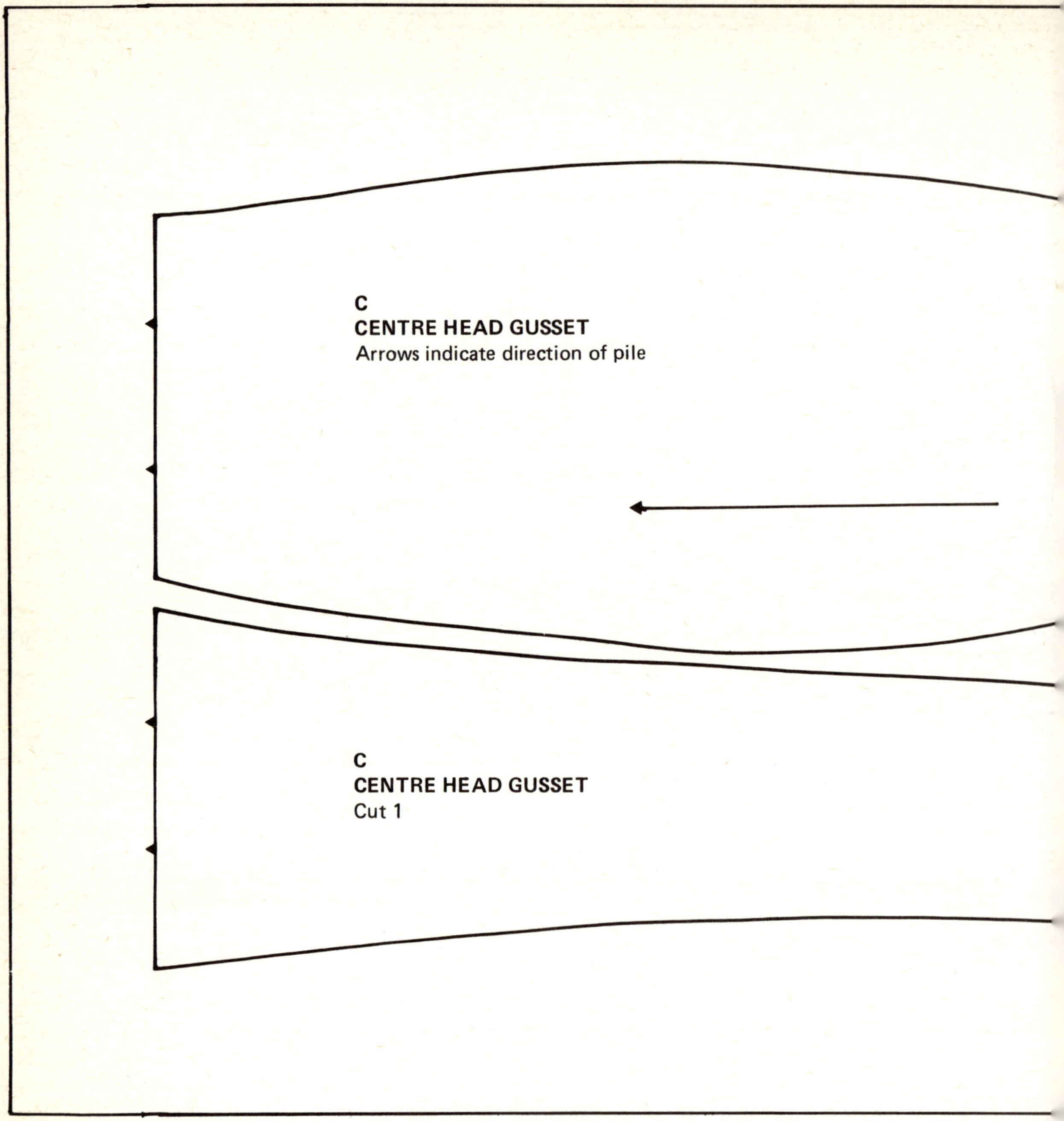

C
CENTRE HEAD GUSSET
Arrows indicate direction of pile

C
CENTRE HEAD GUSSET
Cut 1

straight edge. Trim seam, turn to right side (Fig. 9). Fold in raw edge and pin ears to head (make a small tuck in inner ear of long haired fur) stitch in place.

*A mouth can be made if short pile fur fabric is used. Cut one mouth shape in fur and one in contrast felt. Stitch together leaving open straight edge. Trim seam. Turn to right side. Turn in raw edges and stitch securely in mouth position, folding slightly when stitching (Fig. 10).

*Make a tail by folding in the edges of strip and folding the tail in half. Slip stitch the edges together (Fig. 11). Stitch the tail securely to rear of Mammoth.

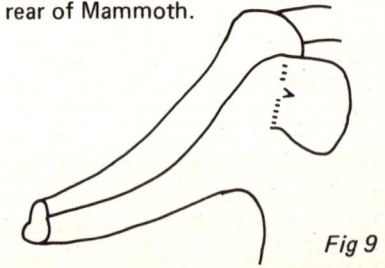

Fig 9

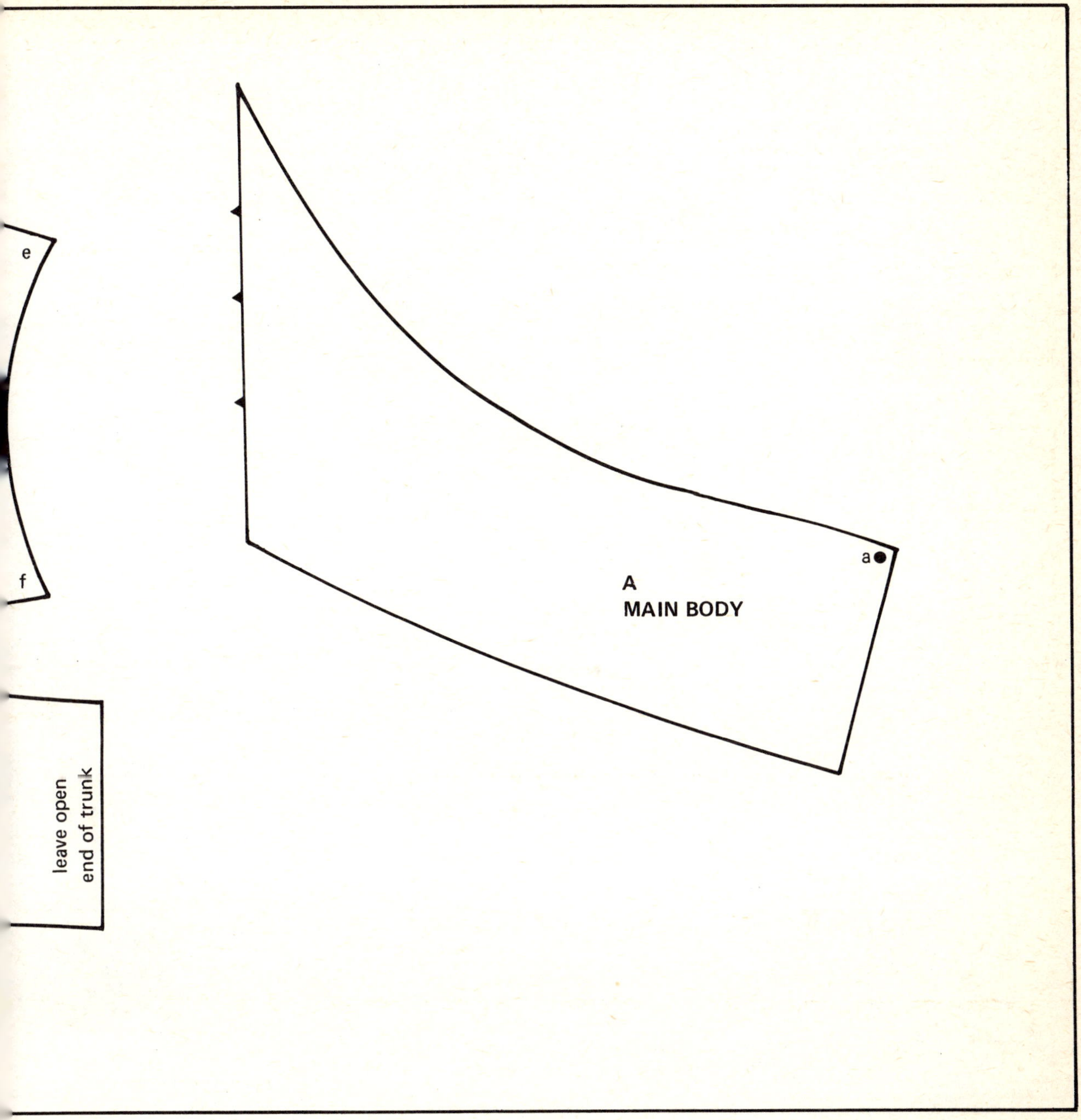

e

f

leave open
end of trunk

a●

A
MAIN BODY

Tusks

*The tusks can be successfully made with a $\frac{1}{2}$in (1.25cm) seam which is either trimmed and left on the outside of the tusk (Fig. 12) or the tusk after seaming is turned inside out, easing it out with the blunt end of a thick knitting needle. This is slightly more difficult but gives a good finish. Match two sections of the tusk together and stitch, leaving ends open. Check stitching on both sides of tusk, to make sure that the seam is secure.

*Stuff tusks inserting a tiny amount of stuffing at a time on the blunt end of the knitting needle, smoothly moulding the tusks into

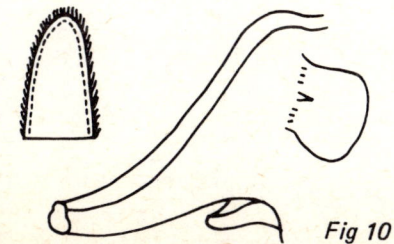

Fig 10

a curve. Fold ends of tusks on fold line. Pin to the side of the head and securely sew into position. A few stitches taken diagonally through the head will keep the tusks raised up (Fig. 13).

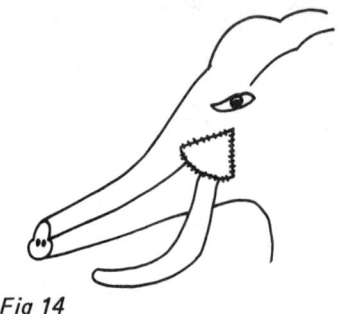

Fig 14

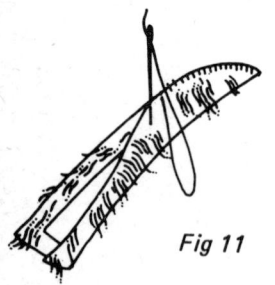

Fig 11

Fig 12

*If plastic eyes have not been used make felt eyes with a small circle of dark felt sewn to the eye backings and stitch to head. Attach nostrils to the nose. These and the eye backings can be glued into place.

*To indicate the head hump and the bridge of the trunk a few hand stitches are made through the head and stuffing (Fig. 15).

Fig 15

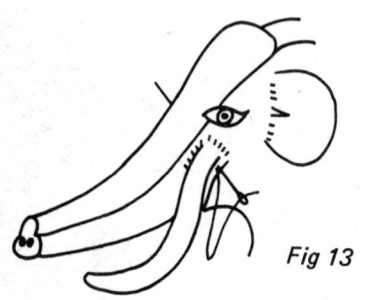

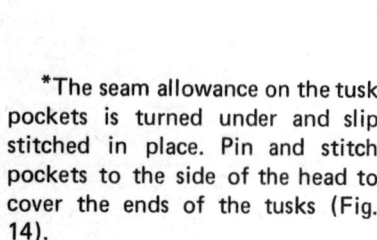

Fig 13

*Brush Mammoth and run a needle along the seams to pull out the 'caught' pile on the fur.

*The seam allowance on the tusk pockets is turned under and slip stitched in place. Pin and stitch pockets to the side of the head to cover the ends of the tusks (Fig. 14).

Plesiosaur: The Loch Ness Monster?

Plesiosaur (nearly-lizard) was another swimming reptile that lived at the same time as the ichthyosaur, 150 million years ago. Its adaptation to life in the water was just as good as the ichthyosaurs, but quite different. It had a long sinuous neck and a round, tubby body. It swam by rowing along with its large paddles, which were so strong that it could probably have crawled out onto the shore. The largest plesiosaurs grew 50 feet long and must have looked magnificent as they swam along. They became extinct about 80 million years ago, though there is a persistent but un-proven myth that some have survived in Loch Ness.

MATERIALS REQUIRED

Main body fabric: 36 x 36ins (90 x 90cm)
Contrast fabric or felt for flipper linings and mouth: 12 x 27ins
White felt for teeth: 3 x 6½ins (7.5 x 16.5cm)
Plastic safety eyes 10mm (optional) or scrap dark felt
Sewing cotton
Stuffing: 8oz (226g)
Size of Model: Length 27ins (67 cm); Height 10ins (25cm)

MAKING-UP

Patterns

Make up patterns as explained in Hints and Instructions. Pieces required are: 2 main bodies (A); 1 under-body (B); 8 flippers (4 pairs) (C); 1 mouth lining (D); 2 eye backings (E); 2 rows teeth (F).

Cutting out

Place pattern pieces on the fabrics, 2 main bodies; 1 under-body and 4 flippers from main fabric. Four flippers, mouth lining and 2 eye backings from contrast. Two rows of teeth from white felt. Mark around patterns and cut out. (Remember to allow turnings appropriate to the fabric as explained in Hints and Instructions.)

Sewing

*Stay-stitch mouth and neck on each piece of main body between 'a' and 'c' (Fig. 1).
*With right sides together match

MOUTH LINING
Cut 1 felt
allow turnings

EYE BACKING
Cut 2

EYE DOTS
Cut 2 each

main bodies together. Pin and stitch from 'a' at mouth, along back and upper tail to 'd' at end of tail. With right side together stitch under-body to main body from 'b' at mouth to tail, easing to fit. Leave open mouth end 'e' to 'b' to form lower jaw. Repeat by stitching the other side of under-body to main

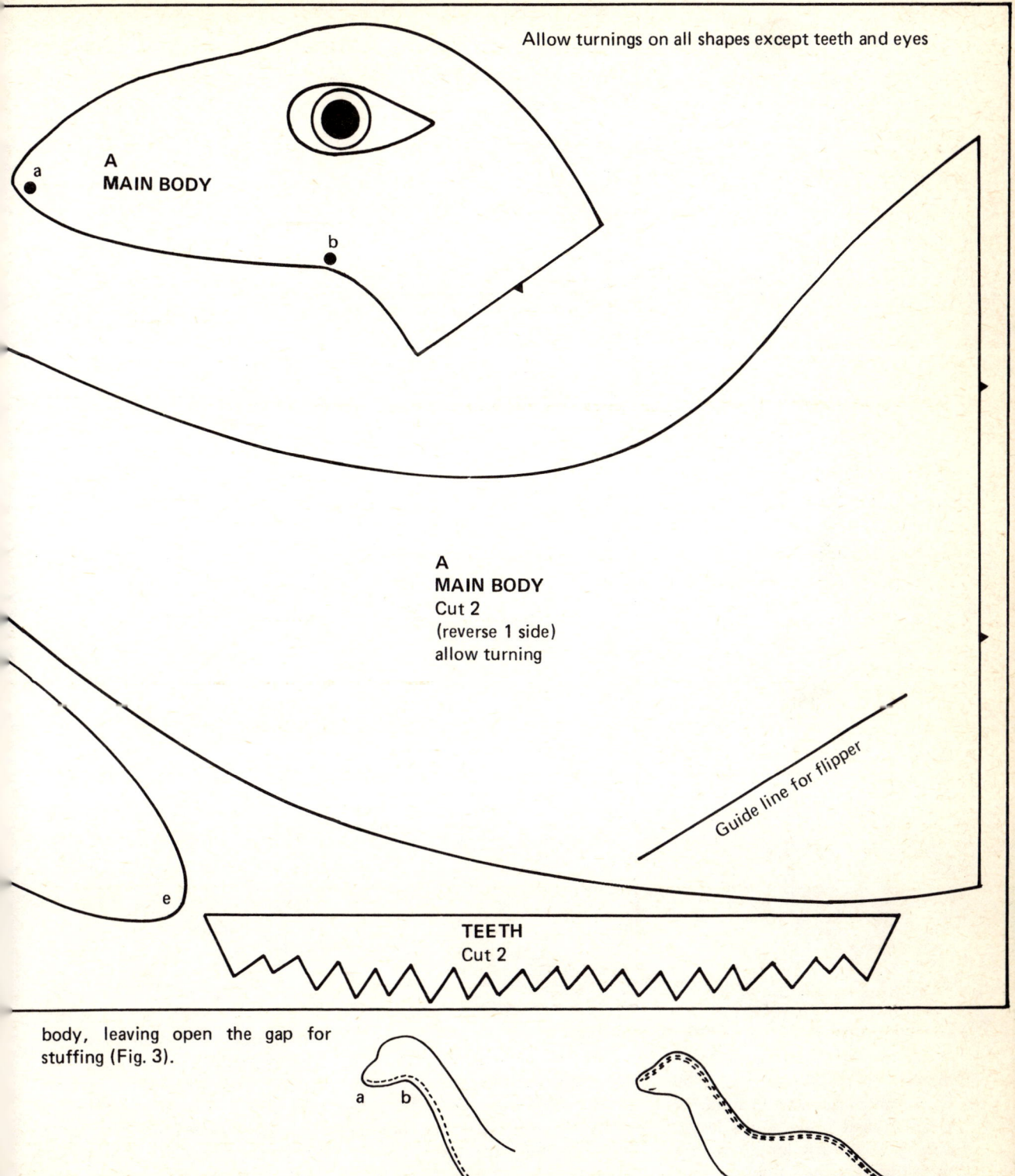

Allow turnings on all shapes except teeth and eyes

A
MAIN BODY

a

b

A
MAIN BODY
Cut 2
(reverse 1 side)
allow turning

Guide line for flipper

e

TEETH
Cut 2

body, leaving open the gap for
stuffing (Fig. 3).

a b

c

Fig 1

Fig 2

*If plastic eyes are to be used then turn the head to the right side, smooth out centre head seam, make a smal! hole in the centre of the eye backing and pin the backing in place on the head. Fix eye as explained in Hints and Instructions.

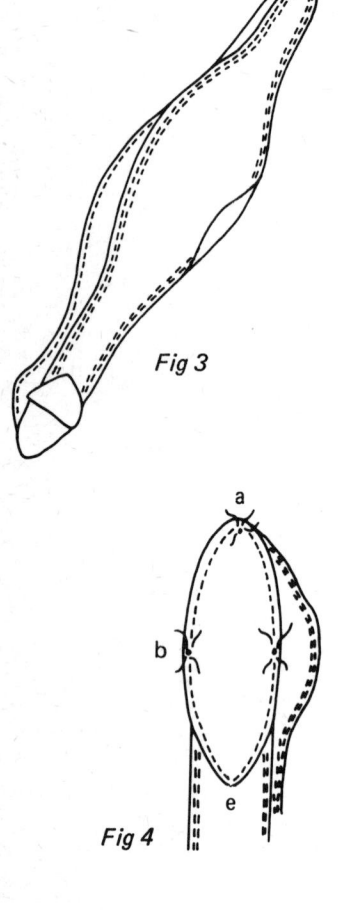

Fig 3

Fig 4

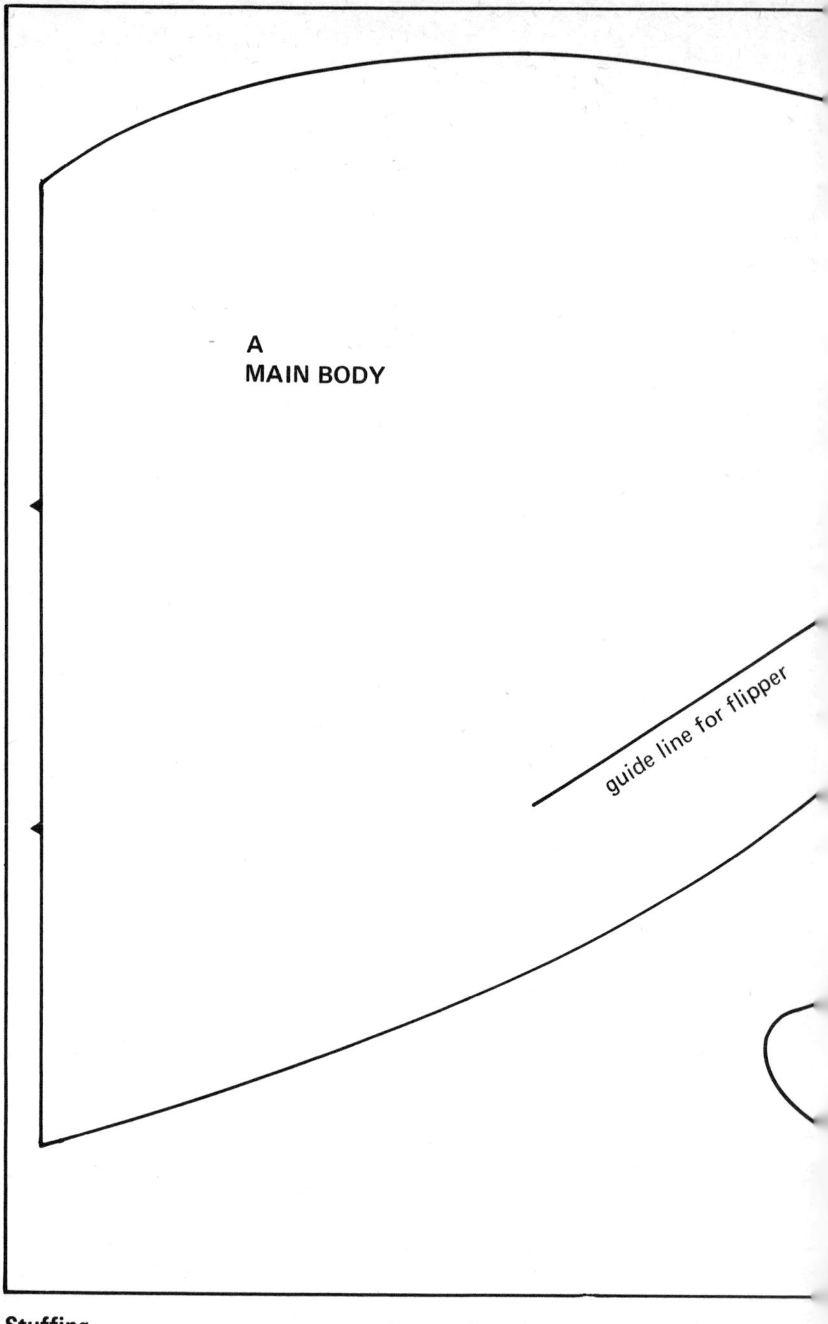

A
MAIN BODY

guide line for flipper

Stuffing

*Fill the creature with stuffing, beginning with the head and lightly fill the lower jaw. Fill the neck firmly (see Hints and Instructions). When the body stuffing is completed close the gap and brush to remove excess filling.

*With right sides together match

*With right sides together pin mouth lining to the head and under-body matching letters. Stitch between 'a' and 'b' on both sides and around under-body mouth 'b' to 'e' to 'b', breaking and securing stitching at 'a' and 'b' (Fig. 4). Turn Plesiosaur to right side out.

two flipper sections together (one main fabric and one contrast). Remember that these must be two pairs (Fig. 5). Pin and stitch, leaving open the straight ends. Trim seams and clip to curves. Turn to the right side out. Press and baste the open edges together (Fig. 6).

*Pin each flipper onto the main

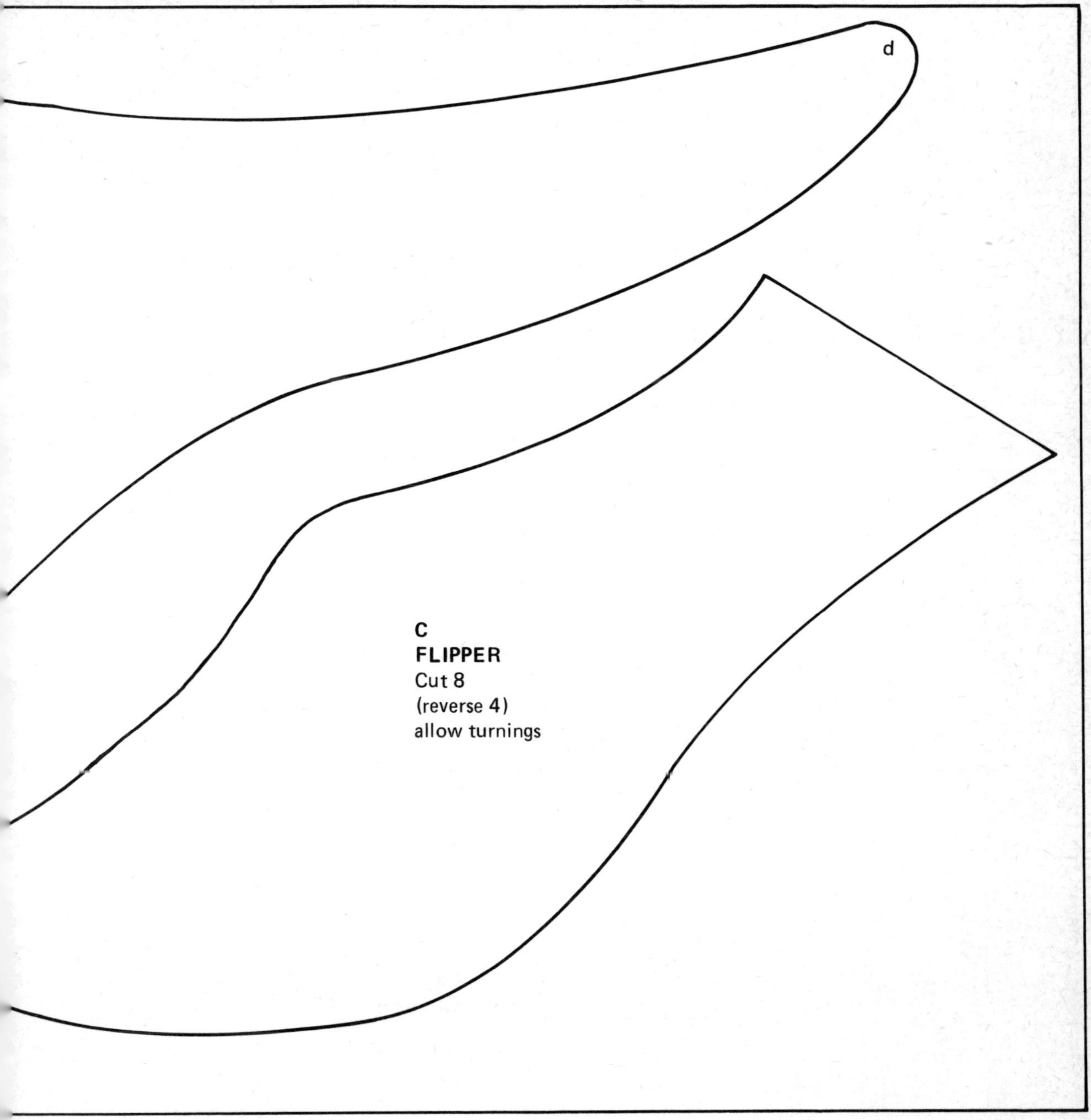

d

C
FLIPPER
Cut 8
(reverse 4)
allow turnings

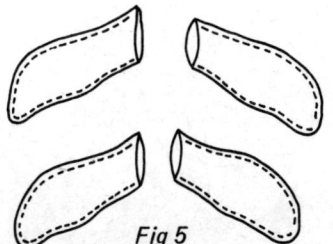

Fig 5

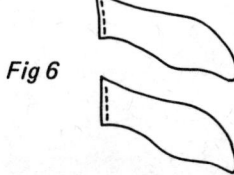

Fig 6

body along guide lines shown on the pattern and stitch in place (Figs. 7 and 8).

Finishing

*If plastic eyes are not used, cut two small dots of black felt and two larger white circles also of felt. Sew a black dot in the centre

55

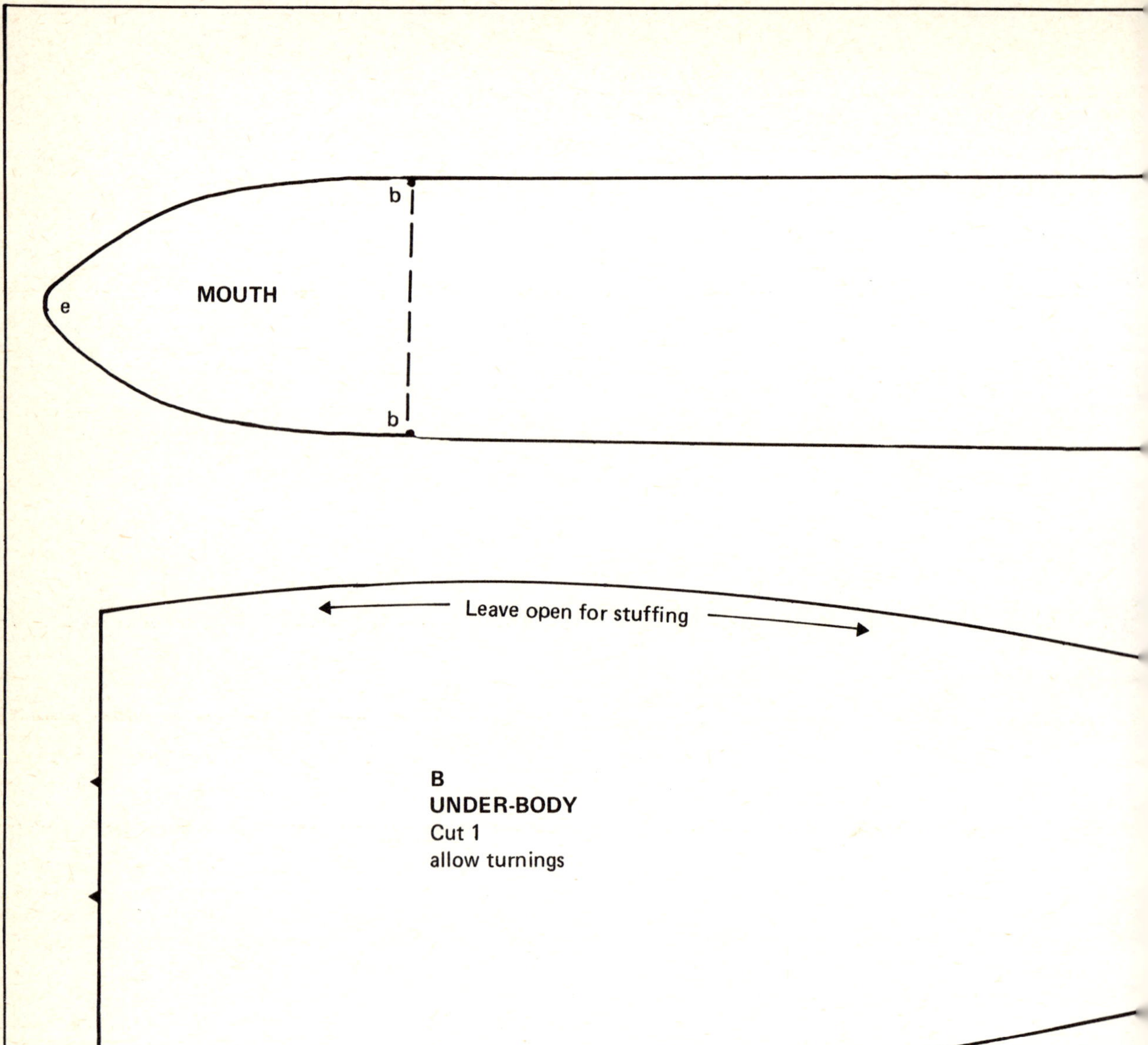

MOUTH

e

b

b

Leave open for stuffing

**B
UNDER-BODY
Cut 1
allow turnings**

of each white circle and then sew each white circle to an eye backing. Sew the eye backing on to the head along the guide lines. Repeat for the other eye. Cut two nostrils of dark felt and attach to head or mark nostrils with a few satin stitches.

*Pin upper and lower rows of teeth to the mouth along the seam

lines, overlapping the ends. Stitch into position (Fig. 9).

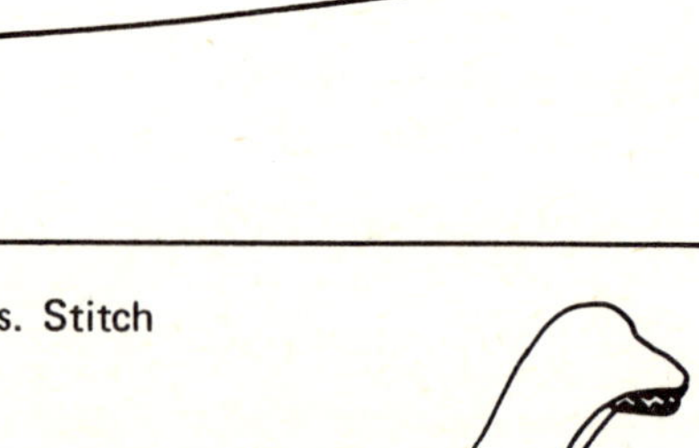

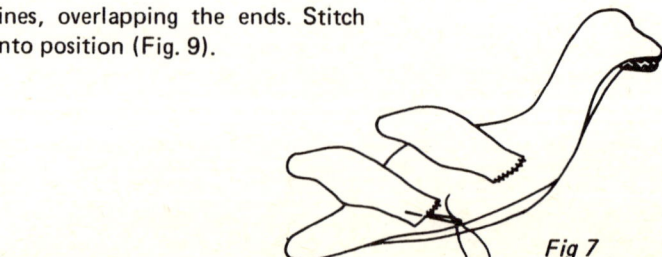

Fig 7

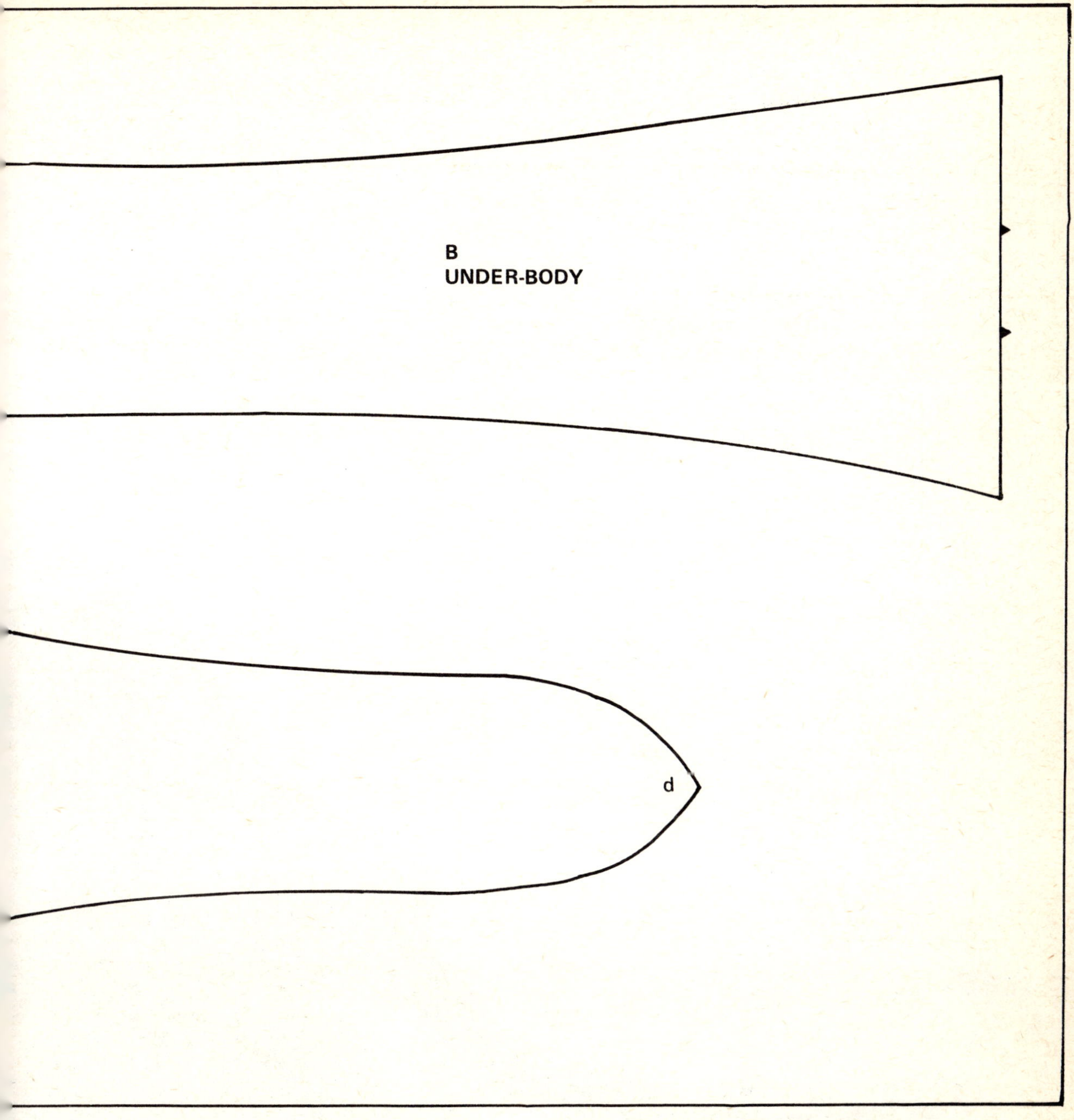

B
UNDER-BODY

d

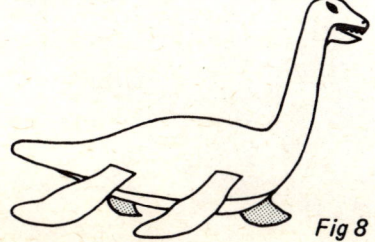

Fig 8

Fig 9

Pteranodon: The Lizard-Bird

A
HALF UPPER BODY
Cut 1

A

I
EYE-BACKING
Cut 2

C

NOSTRIL
Cut 2

a

Pteranodon (wings, no-teeth) was an enormous flying reptile that lived in North America during the Cretaceous Period, 100 million years ago. It was a member of a large group of reptiles that evolved a leathery wing supported on an enormously elongated little finger. *Pteranodon* was the largest of all, having a wingspan of 25 feet (7.5m). It must have been able to glide without effort using rising currents of air, but it probably could not flap its wings much. Its legs were so small and weak that it could not have walked on the surface. Its long toothless beak enabled it to pick fish out of the surface waters as it skimmed along, while the enormous crest must have had some function when the animal was flying. Although unrelated to birds or bats, it has been suggested that Pteranodon was warm blooded and covered with fur. Pteranodon, like all the flying reptiles, died out about 70 million years ago.

MATERIALS REQUIRED

Main body of felt: 22 x 26ins (55 x 65cm)
Red felt for mouth: 4 x 8ins (10 x 20cm)
Vilene for wings: 18 x 32ins (45 x 80cm)
Cold-water dye
Strong but pliable wire: 8ft (2.4m)
10 black pipe cleaners
Sewing cotton
Strong thread
Plastic safety eyes 12mm (optional) or scraps of black and white felt
Scrap yellow felt for eye backing
Stuffing: 6oz (169g)
Clear sticky tape

Wire cutters
Size of Model: Length 15ins (37 cm); Wing span 3ft 6ins (8.75cm)

DYEING

Dye the vilene to your chosen colour. Dry and press.

MAKING-UP

Patterns

Make-up patterns as explained in Hints and Instructions. Pattern shapes required are: 1 upper body (A); 2 under-bodies (B); 2 sides of head (C); 1 centre head gusset (D); 2 lower jaws (E); 1 top mouth lin-ing (F); 1 lower mouth lining (G); 2 wings (H); 2 eye backings (I); 2 nostrils (J). Plus 2 strips for wings $17\frac{1}{2}$ins by $1\frac{3}{4}$ins (43 x 4cm) each.

Cutting out

Lay pattern pieces on to fabrics: 1 upper body; 2 under-bodies;

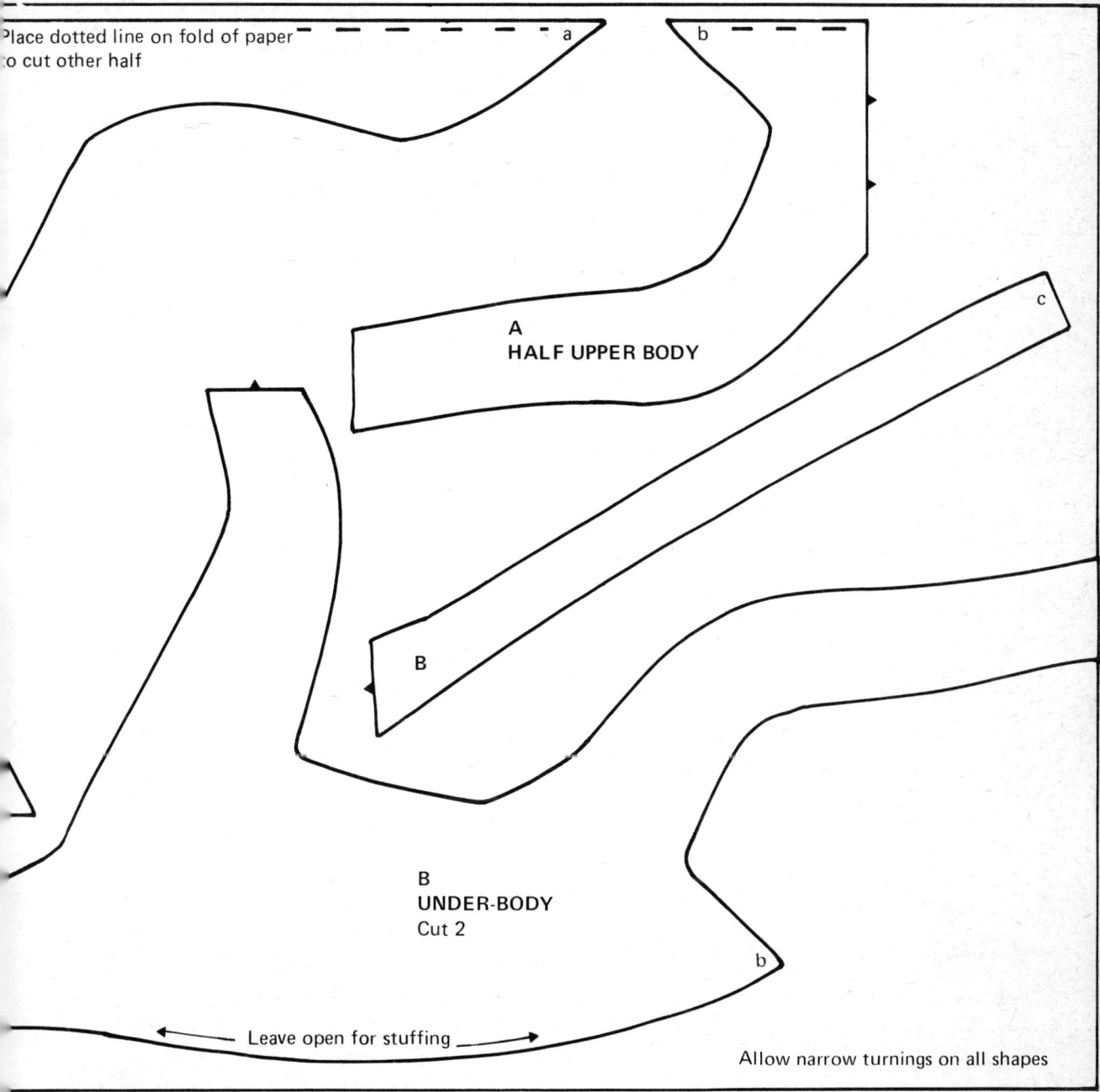

Place dotted line on fold of paper to cut other half

a b

c

A
HALF UPPER BODY

B

B
UNDER-BODY
Cut 2

b

Leave open for stuffing

Allow narrow turnings on all shapes

2 side of head; 1 centre head gusset; 2 lower jaws and wing strips on main body felt. Top and lower mouth linings on red felt. Two wings on Vilene. Two eye backings and two nostrils on yellow and black felt respectively. Cut out following Hints and Instructions.

Sewing

Main body

*Join together the two under-bodies from 'a' at head to 'b' at tail, leaving open centre gap (Fig. 1).

*Match together the body and completed under-body with the under-body seam on the inside. Pin and stitch along upper fore arm around head to other arm at 'c' (Fig. 2). This seam can be made by machine. Put body to one side.

Wings

*Stitch the wings together in centre (Fig. 3).

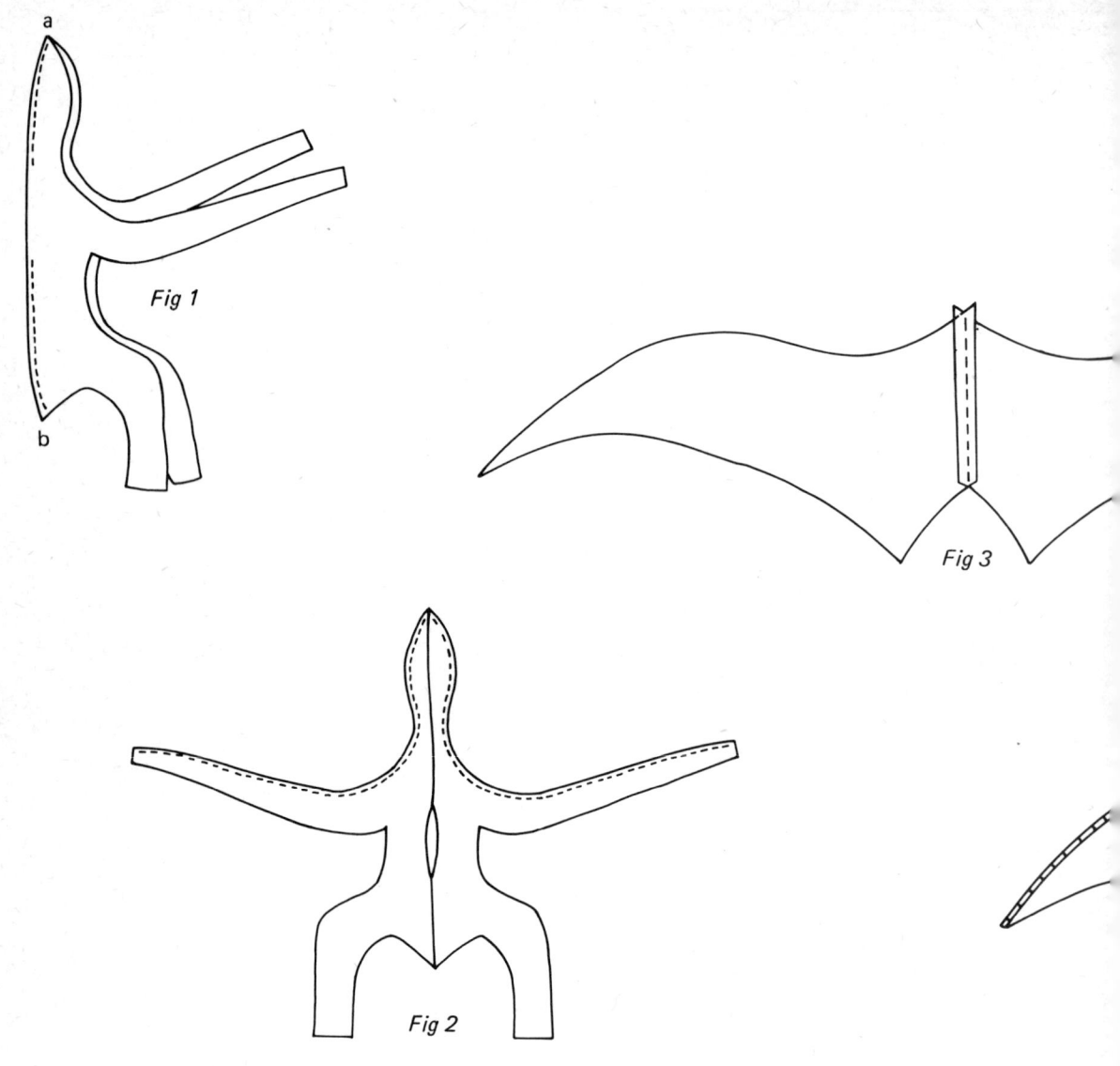

Fig 1

Fig 3

Fig 2

Wire frame

*Cut length of wire in half, bend wire to shape along the upper side of one wing, down the centre of body and around leg position (Fig. 4). Shape the wire for the other side to match. Bind wing end of wire with sticky tape, and bind wire at leg to make safe.

*Beginning at the outside edge and securing with a few stitches through the sticky tape, oversew the wire to wings along the top edge, down the centre of the body to the ends of the legs. Check leg position by laying the body shape on the top of the wings. Oversew the two wires together in the centre of the body.

Feet and claws

*Make feet and claws with two pipecleaners folded in half plus half a pipe cleaner twisted together (Fig. 5). The pipe cleaners can be painted or dyed to required colour. Put claws to one side.

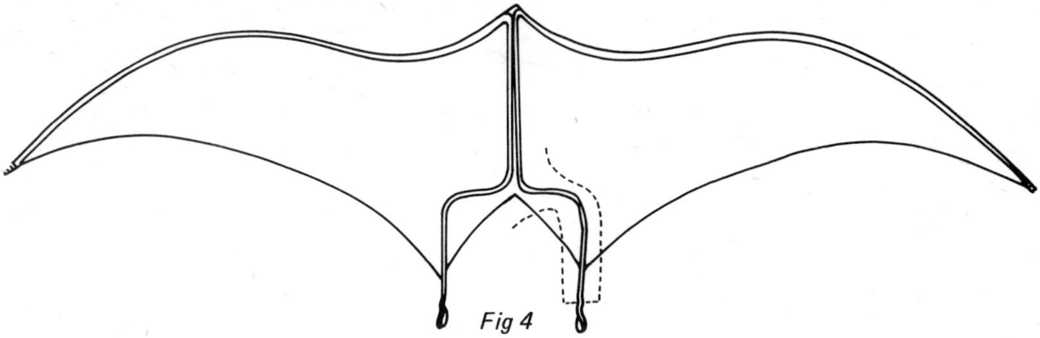

Fig 4

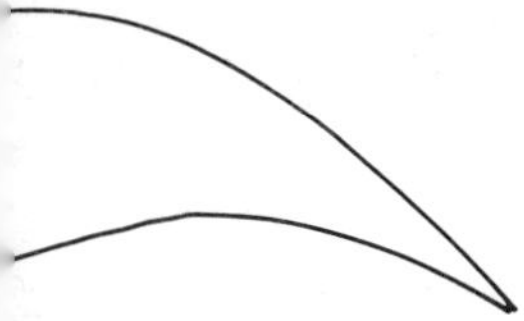

Fig 5

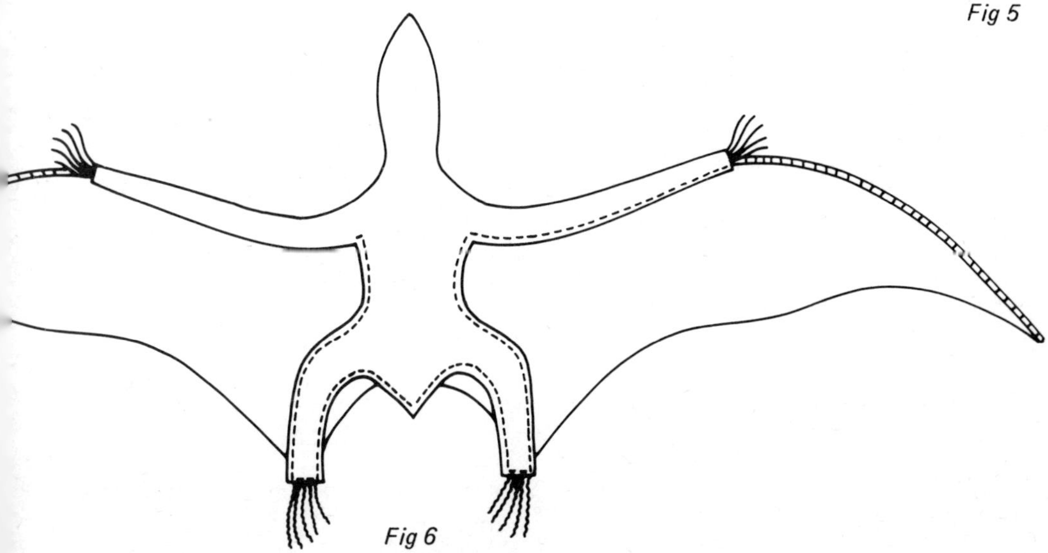

Fig 6

Body and wings

*Place the wings and wire frame between the two body shapes. Pin in place all around upper arms to 'c', body and legs.

*Stab-stitch body to wings (Fig. 6). Before stitching the ends of the legs and fore arms, attach a set of claws to the wire frame (Figs. 7 and 8). Also while stitching, push a little stuffing into the upper side of the body between the felt and the wings as this will be impossible at a later stage.

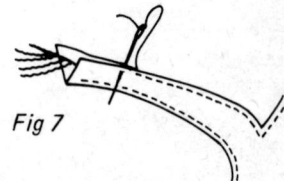

Fig 7

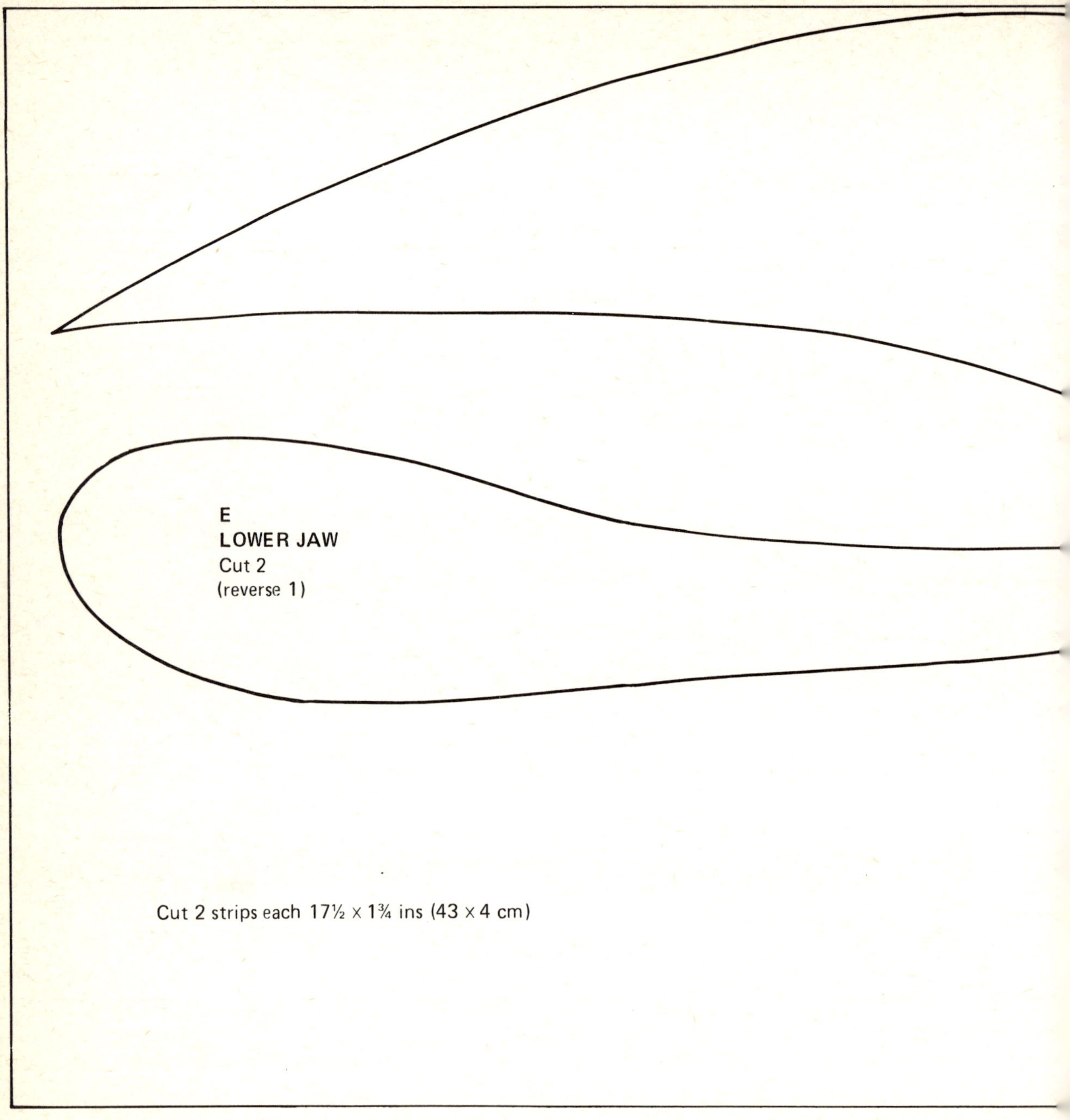

**E
LOWER JAW
Cut 2
(reverse 1)**

Cut 2 strips each 17½ × 1¾ ins (43 × 4 cm)

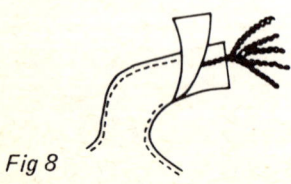

Fig 8

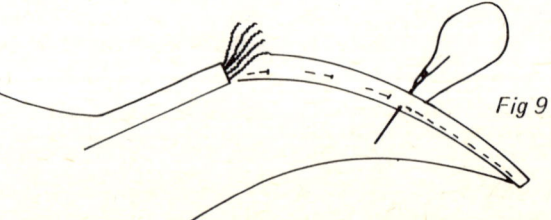

Fig 9

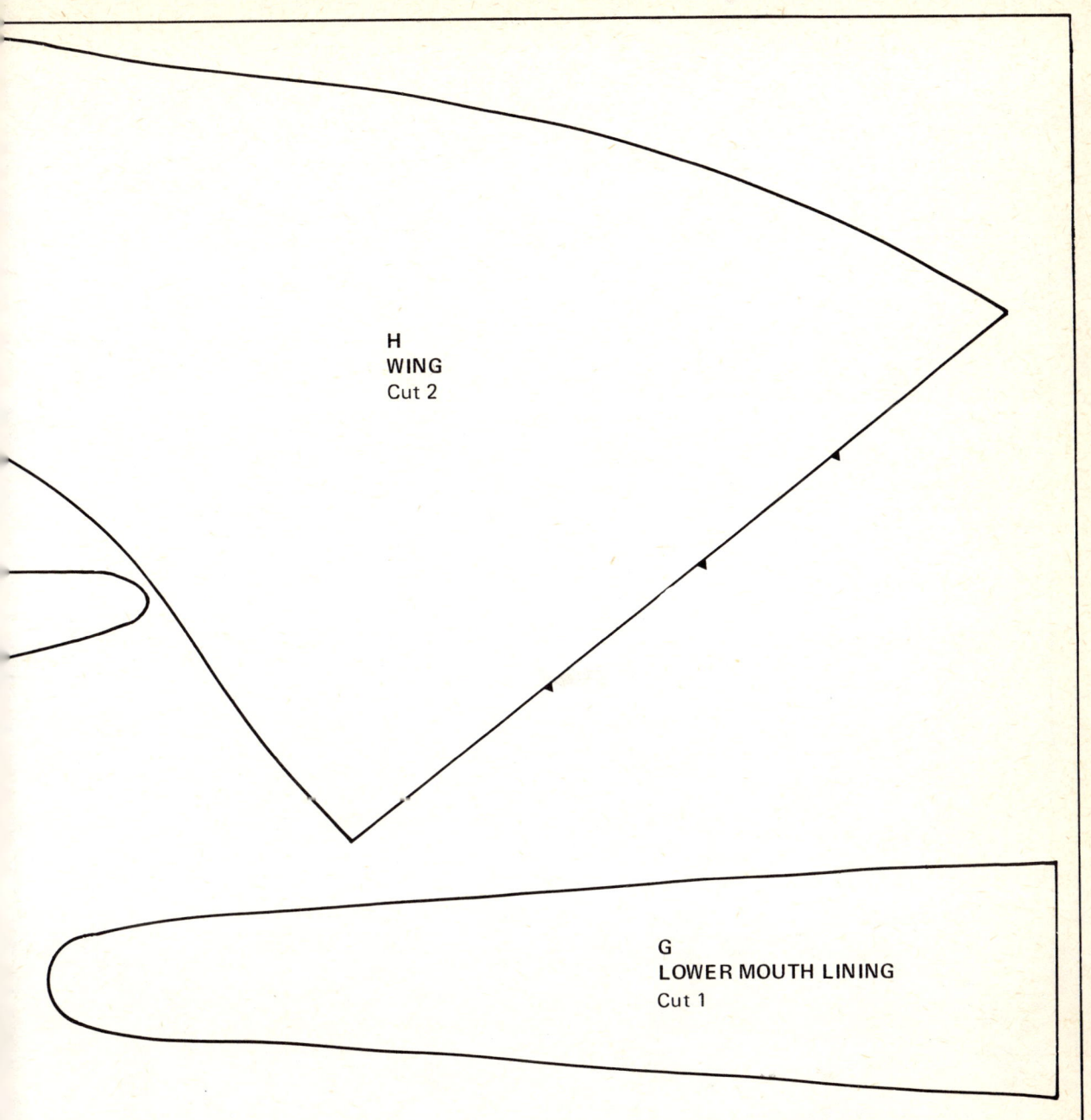

H
WING
Cut 2

G
LOWER MOUTH LINING
Cut 1

Upper ends of wings

*Fold one strip of felt in half. Pin in place along upper edge of wing, joining it to the body fore arm under the claw. Stab-stitch the strip in place as close as possible to the wire. Trim edges of seam to $\frac{1}{8}$in (0.3cm). Repeat for other side of wing (Fig. 9). If a small amount of wing shows between the shoulder and fore arm this too can have a narrow strip stitched over the wire.

Stuffing

*Begin by easing a little stuffing into the legs. Fill the head and body. Close the gap and brush to remove excess stuffing.

Making the head

*Stitch centre gusset to both sides of the head, matching 'e' at nose and 'f' at end of crest. Break and secure stitching at both ends (Fig. 10).

*Pin together edges of crest of head, stitch to 'g'. Pin and stitch top mouth lining to head (Fig. 11).

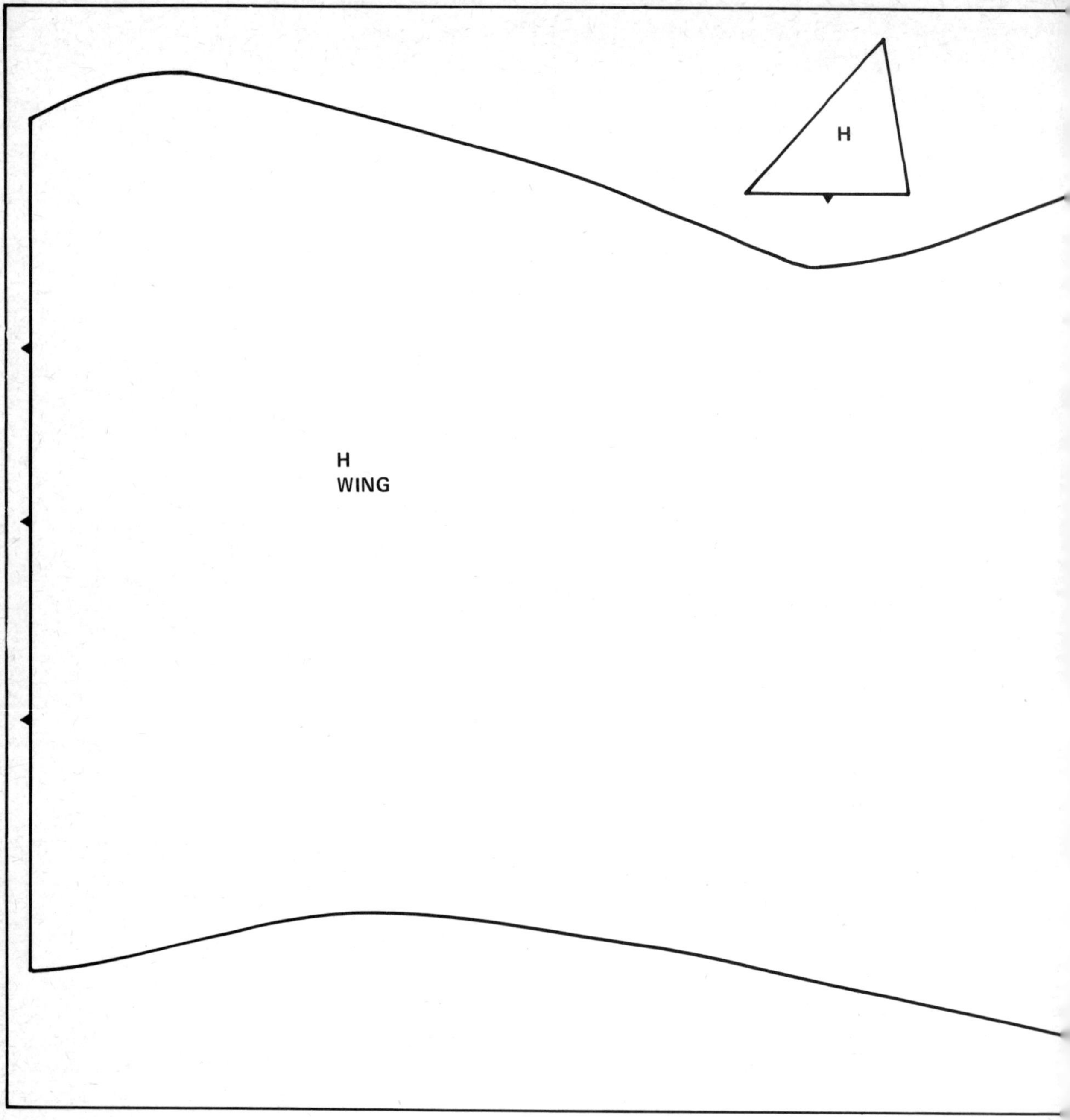

H

H
WING

Turn head to right side out.

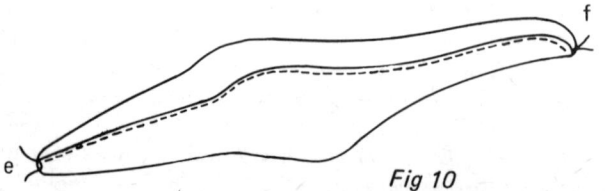

Fig 10

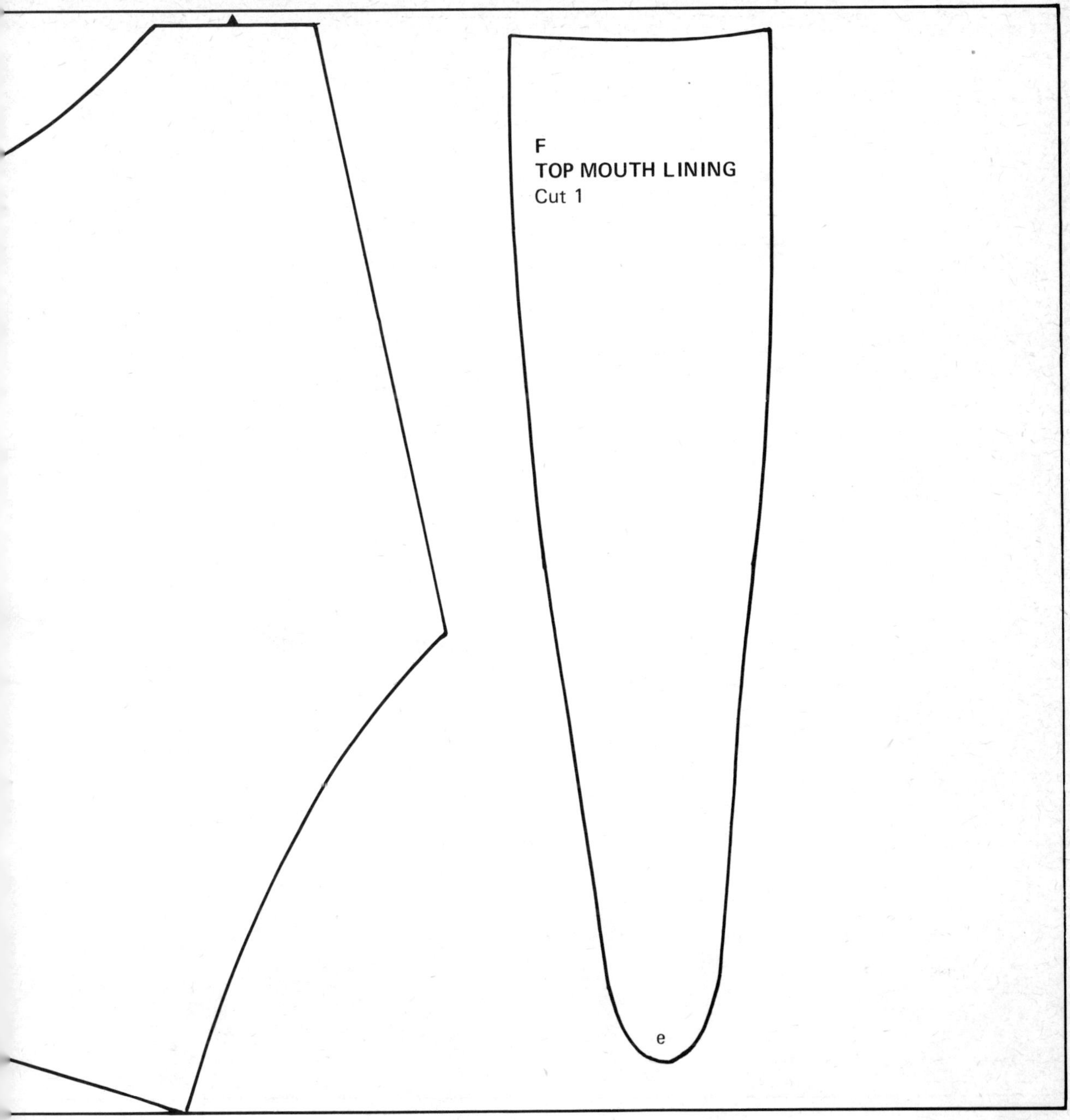

F
TOP MOUTH LINING
Cut 1

e

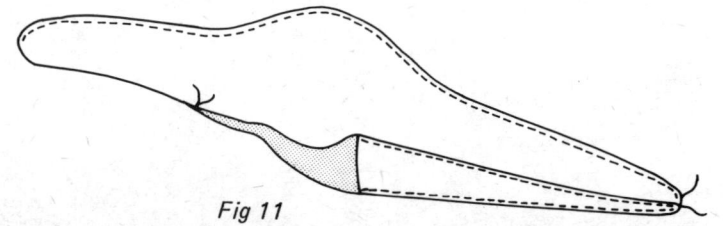

Fig 11

Eyes

*If a plastic eye is to be used, position eye backings on the head and fix eyes following Hints and Instructions.

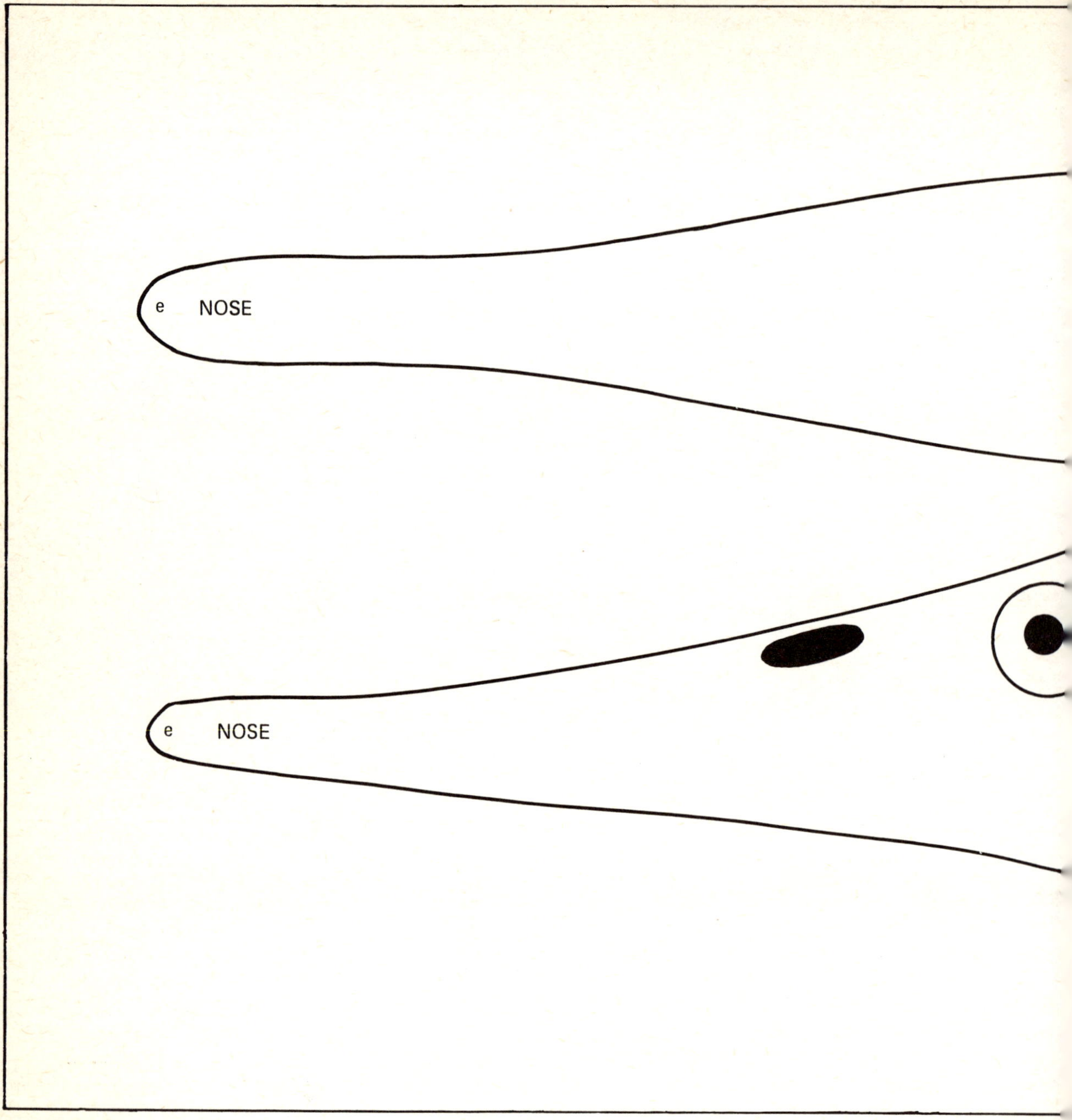

e   NOSE

e   NOSE

Lower Jaw

   *Stitch both lower jaw shapes together. With right sides together, stitch lower mouth lining to jaw (Fig. 12). Turn jaw right side out.

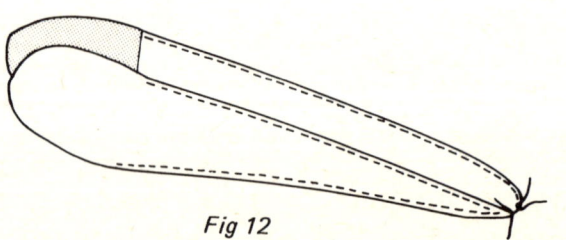

Fig 12

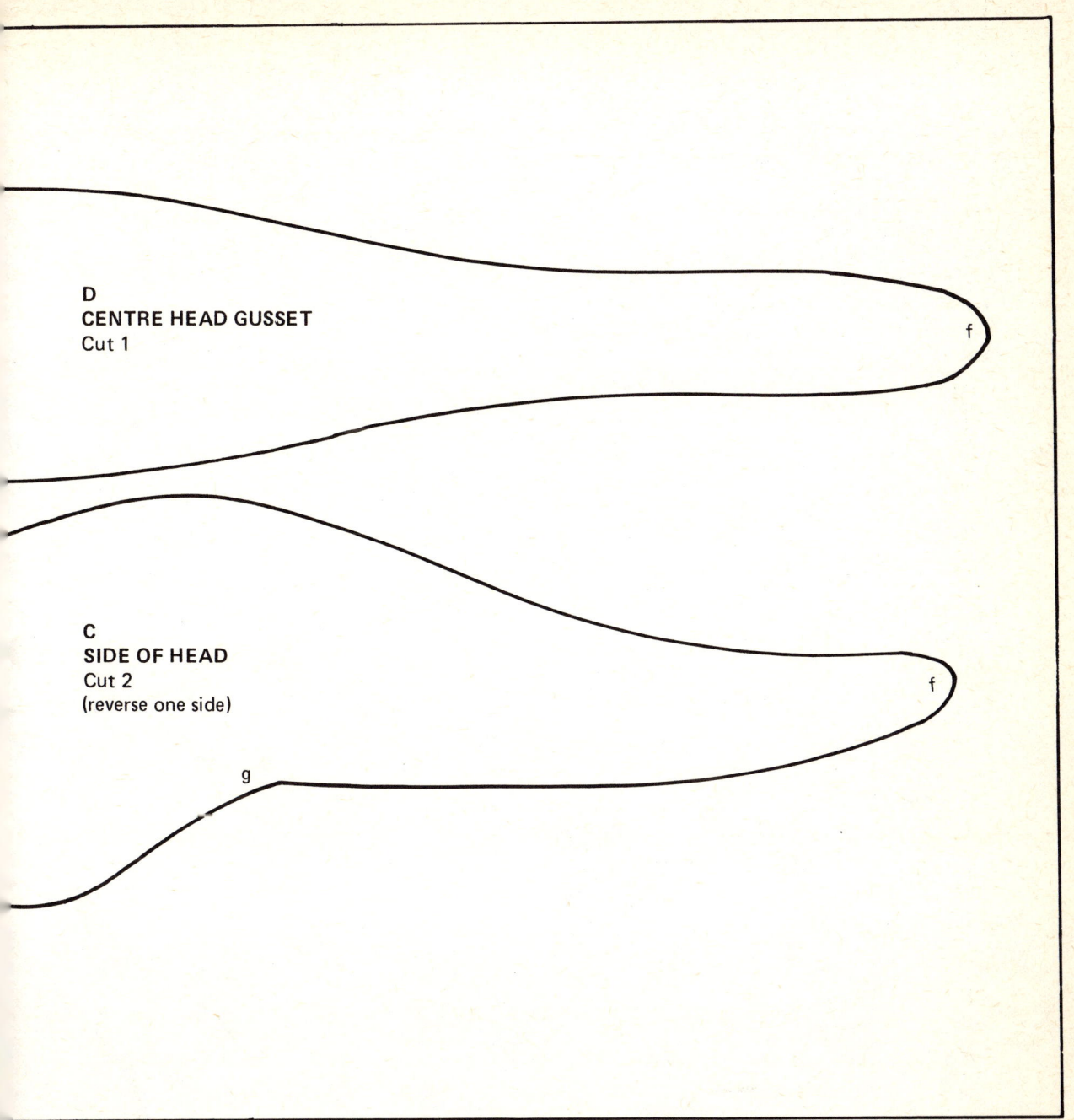

D
CENTRE HEAD GUSSET
Cut 1

f

C
SIDE OF HEAD
Cut 2
(reverse one side)

g

f

Head to lower jaw

*On the inside of the head, over-sew together the open ends of the mouth linings (Fig. 13).

*Lightly fill both head and jaw with stuffing.

Head and neck to body

*Place the head over the head/ neck stump on main body, adjusting the stuffing. The open end of the lower jaw is tucked under the side of the head. Pin in place, check the angle of the head and jaw and stitch to neck. A few stitches can be taken through the neck around the wire frame to hold the neck firmly (Fig. 14).

Finishing

*If plastic eyes have not been used, cut two small dots of black felt and two larger circles of white felt. Stitch these to the eye backing. Place the eyes in position on the Pteranodon and stitch to head. A few stitches taken through the head with the needle coming out

close to the eyes will model the
head with the needle coming out
close eo the eyes will model the
head and give a 'sharper' look to
the creature. Cut nostrils in black
felt and stitch in place, also with
stitches through the head.

Note: The Pteranodon can be
suspended with thread attached
to the upper wings and legs, taking
the thread round the wire frame for
strength.

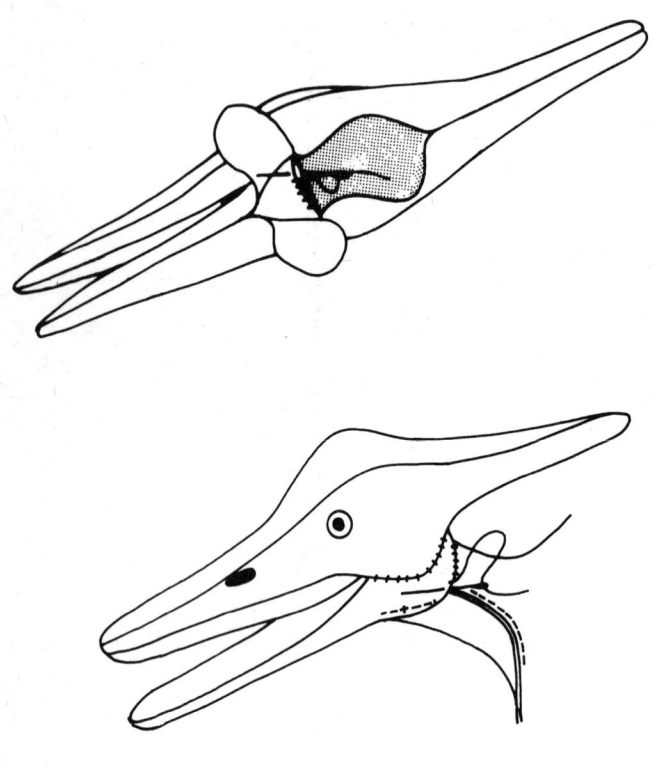

Stegosaurus: Armour-Plated Lizard

EYE BACKI
Cut 2
no turnings

Stegosaurus (plated-lizard) was a large, ungainly plant-eating dinosaur that lived in North America and Europe in the Jurassic Period, 150 million years ago. It had an enormous body supported on short pillar-like legs, and a very small head. Its teeth and jaws were adapted for chewing the leaves and stems of soft plants. Its brain was smaller than that of a modern collie dog, even though Stegosaurus was 20 feet (6m) long and must have weighed several tons. The most remarkable feature of this animal was the double row of triangular plates which ran down its back, presumably protecting the backbone and spinal cord. Two pairs of sharp spines on the tail must have given the animal a little more protection against meat-eaters.

MATERIALS REQUIRED

Main body fabric (felt): 36 x 20ins (90 x 50cm)

Contrast felt (See note): 18 x 14ins (46 x 35cm)

Plastic safety eyes 8mm (optional) or scrap black felt

Embroidery thread

Sewing cotton

Stuffing: 12oz (340g)

Size of Model: Length 18ins (45 cm); Height 7ins (17cm)

Note: A lightweight felt should not be used for the contrast as the back plates need some stiffness.

MAKING-UP

Patterns

Make up patterns as explained in Hints and Instructions. Pieces required are: 2 main body (A); 2 under-body (B); 1 each of plates (C) and (D); 4 leg circles (E); 4 front foot pads (F); 4 rear foot pads (G); 2 eye backings (H).

Cutting out

Place patterns on to fabric, main bodies, under-body and leg circles on main body fabric. Remainder on contrast felt. Mark round the patterns and cut out, remembering to allow for turnings as explained in Hints and Instructions.

Sewing

*Stay stitch along curved lower edges of both sets of plates and then baste both sets together (Fig. 1).

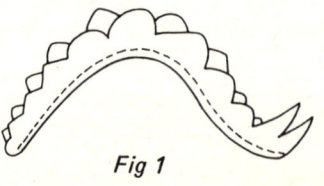

Fig 1

D
PLATES
Cut 1 felt
no turnings

D

*Pin and baste curved lower edge of plates to one side of the main body back, laying them on the right side of the fabric (Fig. 2).

*With right sides together match and pin the other main body shape over the plates. Stitch main bodies together from 'a' at nose along the back to 'd' at tail. Trim seam.

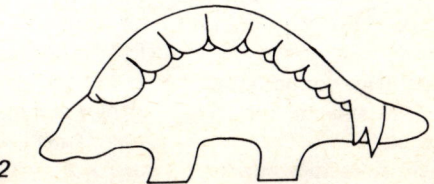

Fig 2

73

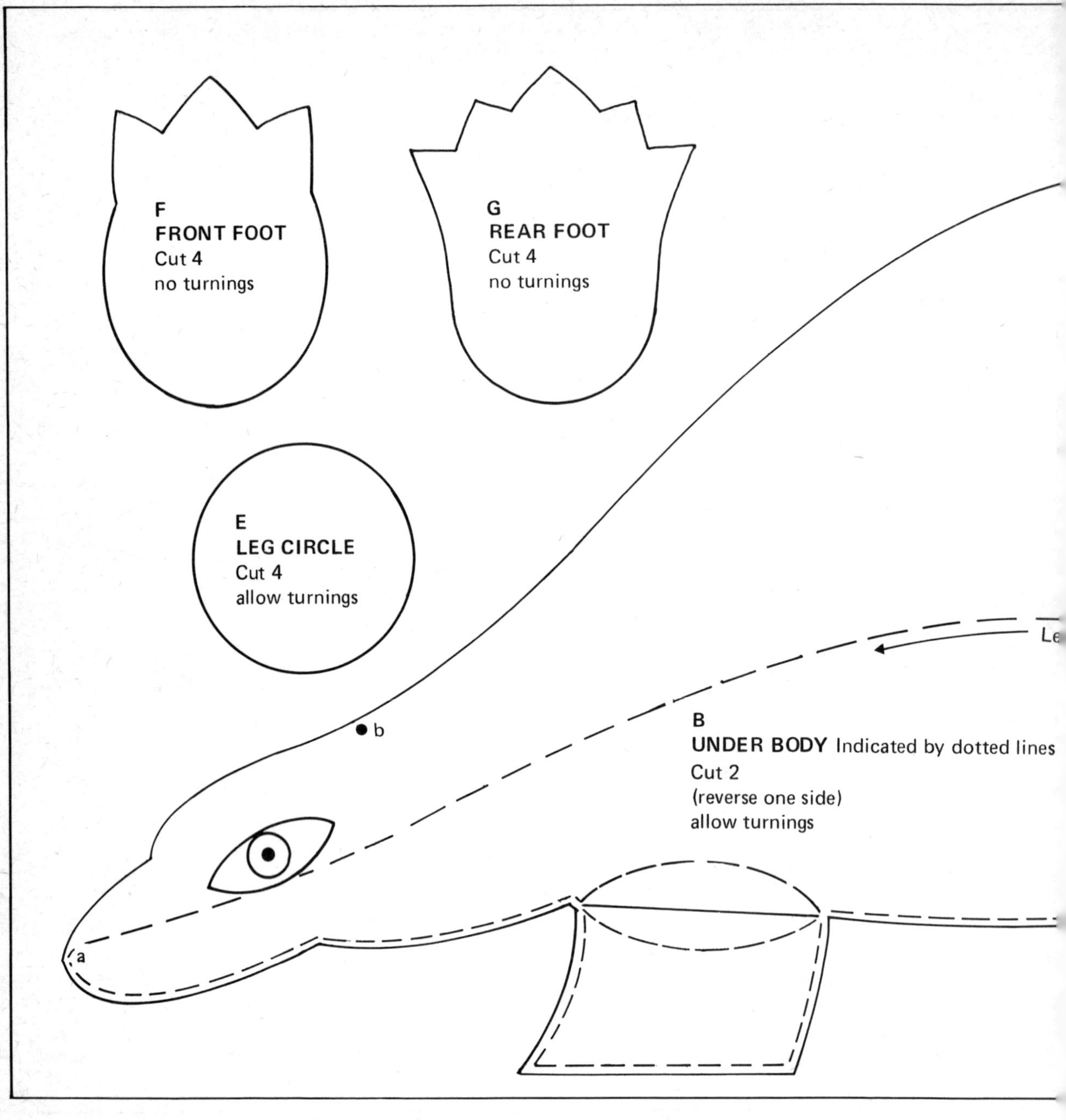

F
FRONT FOOT
Cut 4
no turnings

G
REAR FOOT
Cut 4
no turnings

E
LEG CIRCLE
Cut 4
allow turnings

Le

• b

B
UNDER BODY Indicated by dotted lines
Cut 2
(reverse one side)
allow turnings

a

*If plastic eyes are used, turn head to right side, smooth out centre seam, position eye backings and attach eyes following Hints and Instructions.

*Make arcs in legs of both under-body sections as explained in Hints and Instructions.

*With right sides together stitch one under-body to one side of main body from nose 'a' to tail 'd' leaving open the ends of the legs. Repeat for other under-body (Fig. 3). Trim seams and clip to curves.

*Stitch both under-bodies together along centre seam, leaving open gap for stuffing and taking care not to catch the plates in the seam.

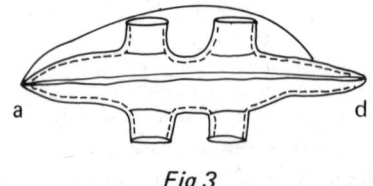

a   d

Fig 3

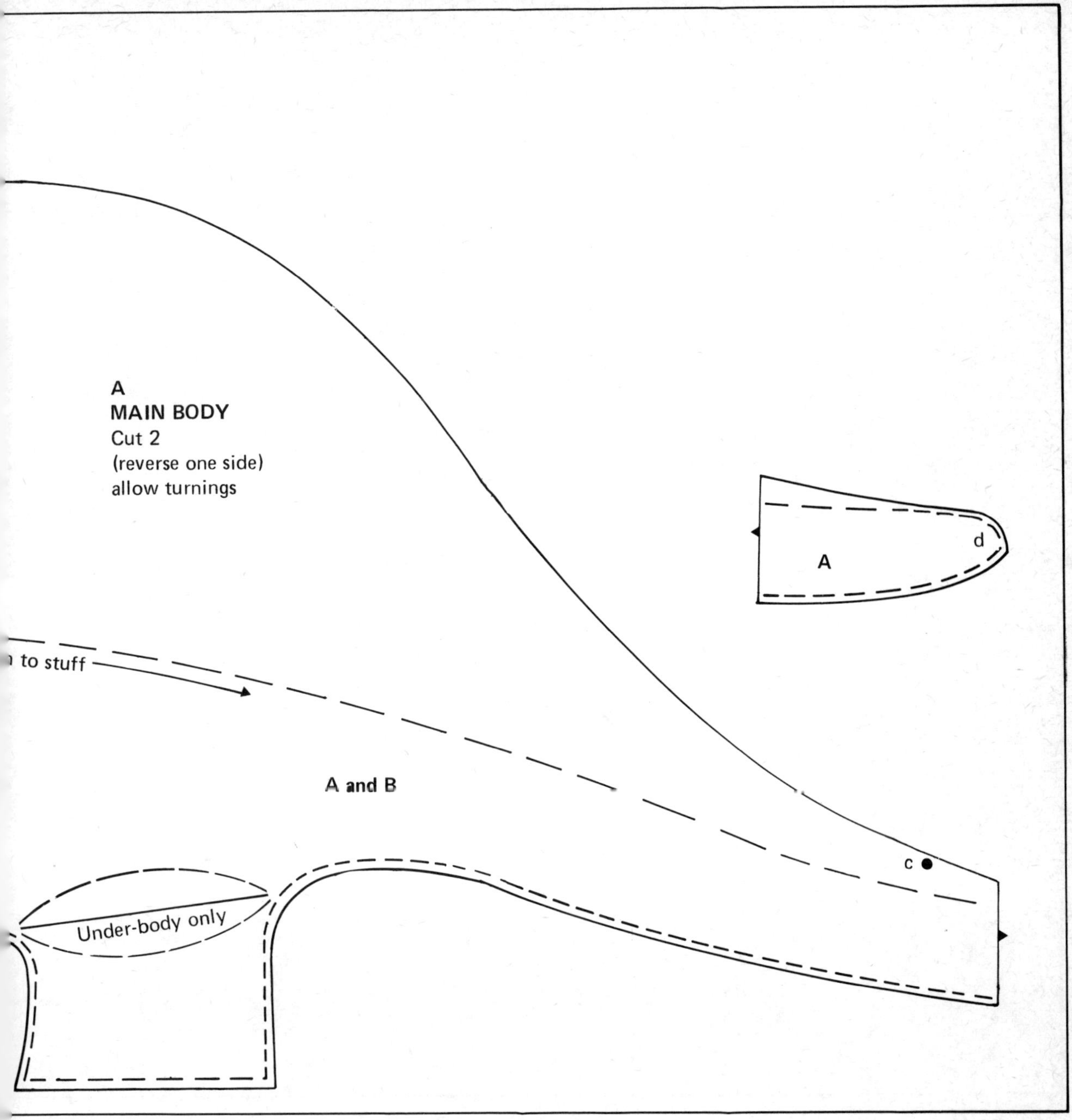

A
MAIN BODY
Cut 2
(reverse one side)
allow turnings

A

d

to stuff

A and B

Under-body only

c ●

*Trim foot circles to size and oversew to ends of legs (Fig. 4).

*Check that no pins are left in the fabric, turn Stegosaurus to right side out.

*Fill carefully with stuffing. Mould the filling into the back and at the same time ensure that the plates are upright. Fill the legs care- fully and when stuffing is comple- ted close the gap and brush to re- move excess stuffing etc.

*Match and top stitch two foot shapes together (Fig. 5). Repeat for the other feet, making two pairs. Slip stitch three toed feet to ends of the front legs and five-toed feet to rear legs (Fig. 6).

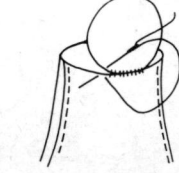

Fig 4

**C
PLATES**
Cut 1 felt
no turnings

*If plastic eyes have not been used then cut two eye dots from the dark felt and stitch them with the eye backings to the head. Embroider the mouth in chain stitch with fine darning wool or cotton and work a few satin stitches to mark the nostrils (Fig. 7).

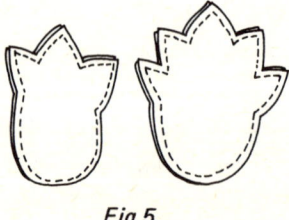

Fig 5

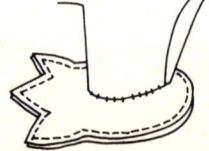

Fig 6

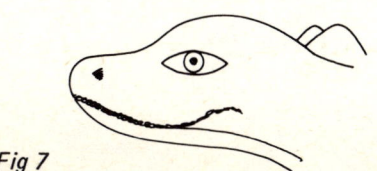

Fig 7

Triceratops: Three-Horned Dinosaur

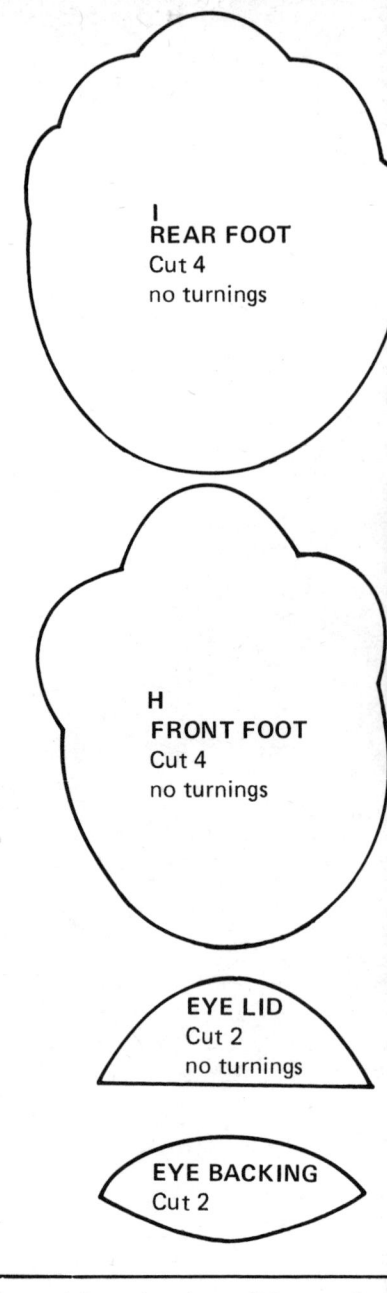

I
REAR FOOT
Cut 4
no turnings

H
FRONT FOOT
Cut 4
no turnings

EYE LID
Cut 2
no turnings

EYE BACKING
Cut 2

Triceratops (three-horned-face) was a large plant-eating dinosaur that lived in North America during the Cretaceous Period, 100 million years ago. This monster, 20 feet (6m) long and 8 feet (2.4m) tall, weighed 8 tons (812kg), about the same as one of the tanks that fought in World War I. As protection against animals like Tyrannosaurus, it had three sharp horns and a heavy bony frill forming part of its skull. It had teeth adapted for crushing tough and fibrous vegetable matter. Although Triceratops was warm-blooded and may even have developed fur in cold places, it was in fact a reptile and laid eggs, quite unlike the rhinoceros that it so closely resembles. Like the other dinosaurs, Triceratops died out about 70 million years ago leaving no descendants.

MATERIALS REQUIRED

Main body fabric: 36 x 28ins (90 x 70cm)
Contrast felt: 12 x 40ins (30 x 100 cm)
Plastic safety eyes 12mm (optional) or scrap of white felt
Scrap of black felt
Sewing cotton
Strong thread
Stuffing: 12oz (339g)
Size of Model: Length 22ins (55 cm); Height 10ins (25cm)

MAKING-UP

Patterns

Make up patterns as explained in Hints and Instructions. Pieces required are: 2 main bodies (A); 2 under-bodies (B); 4 leg circles (C); 2 centre panels for head mask (D); 2 side panels for head mask (E); 2 frill linings (F); 4 under-chin shapes (G); 4 front foot shapes (H); 4 rear foot shapes (I); 2 nostrils (J).

Cutting out

Place pattern pieces on the fabrics. Two main bodies, 2 under-bodies and 4 leg circles on main body fabric. Remainder on contrast felt.

Sewing

Body

*With right sides of material together pin both main body shapes together and stitch around back

from 'a' at head to 'b' at tail (Fig. 1). Trim seam.

*Make leg arcs in both under-bodies following Hints and Instructions notes.

*Right sides together pin and stitch each under-body to each side of main body, leaving open the ends of the legs (Fig. 2). Stitch together

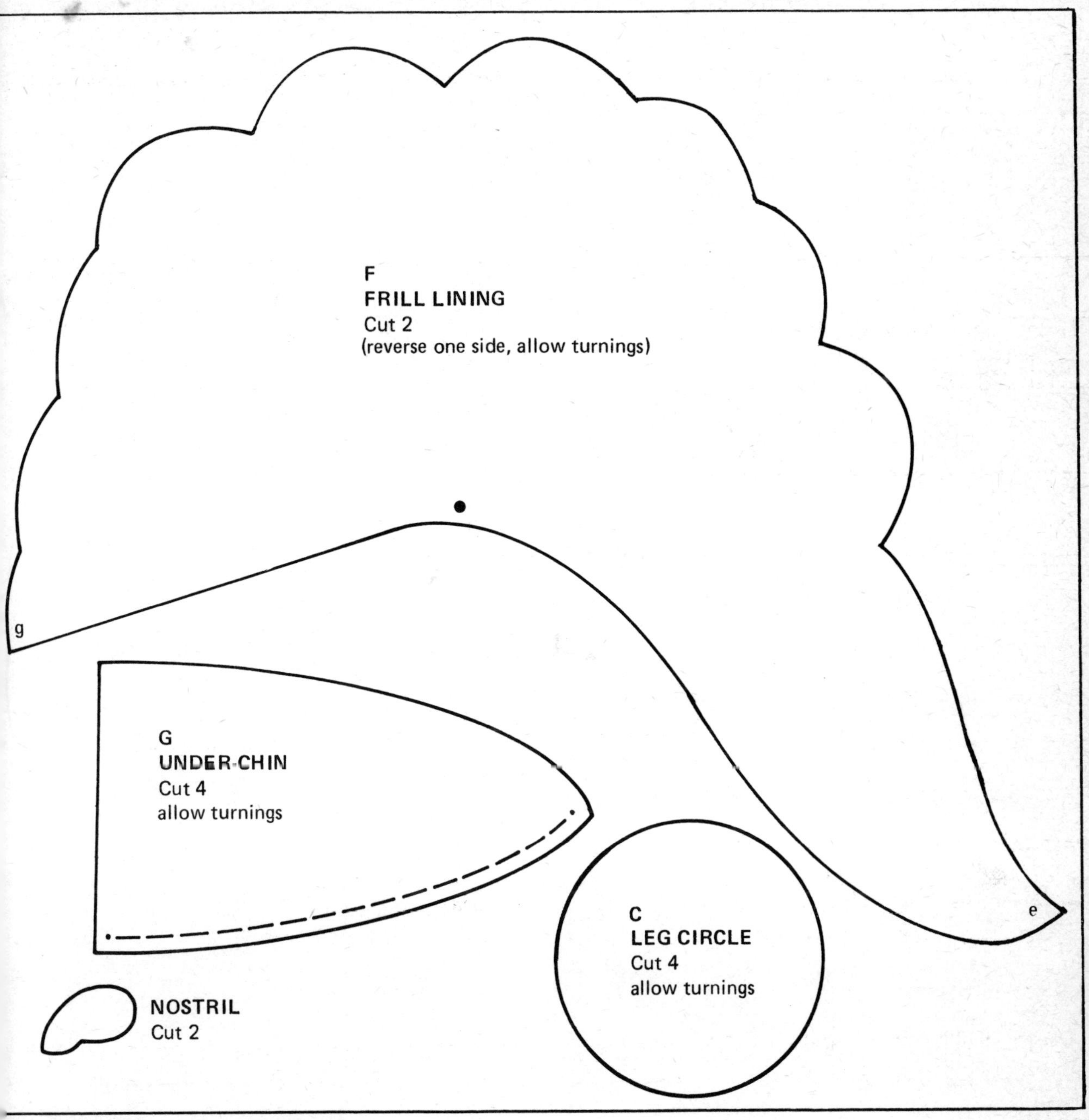

**F
FRILL LINING
Cut 2
(reverse one side, allow turnings)**

g

**G
UNDER-CHIN
Cut 4
allow turnings**

**NOSTRIL
Cut 2**

**C
LEG CIRCLE
Cut 4
allow turnings**

e

the centre seam of under-bodies
from head to tail, leaving open gap
for stuffing. Trim seams and clip to
curves.

   *Pin foot circles to ends of legs
and stitch following Hints and
Instructions.

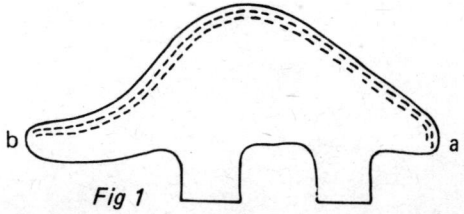

b   a

Fig 1

M.P.P.—F

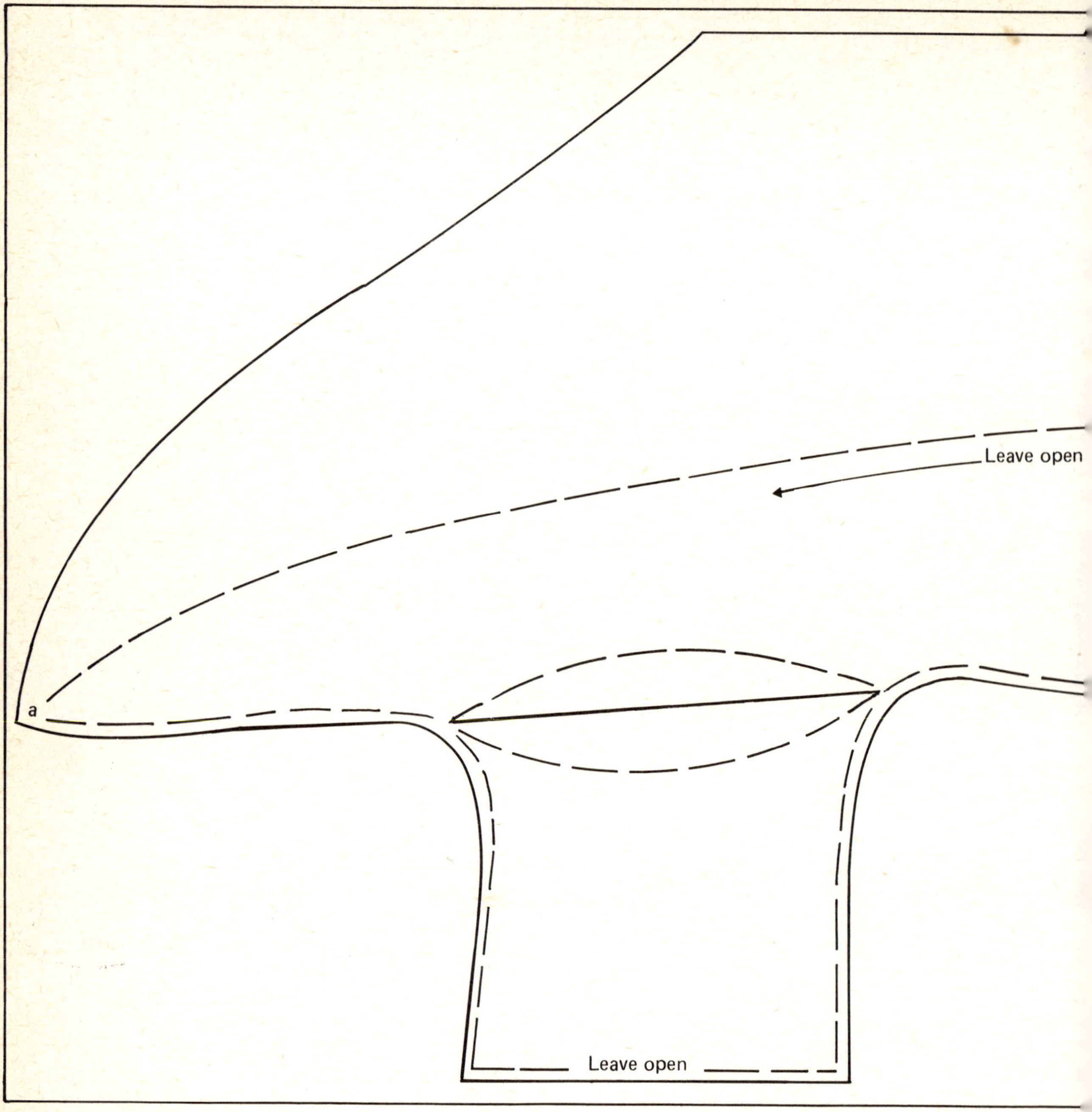

Leave open

a

Leave open

*Check that no pins are left in fabric. Turn Triceratops to right side out.

*Fill the body with stuffing, moulding it into the back hump. When the legs and body are firmly filled, close the gap and brush to remove excess filling.

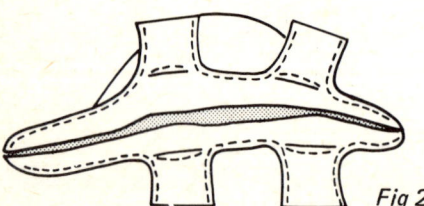

Fig 2

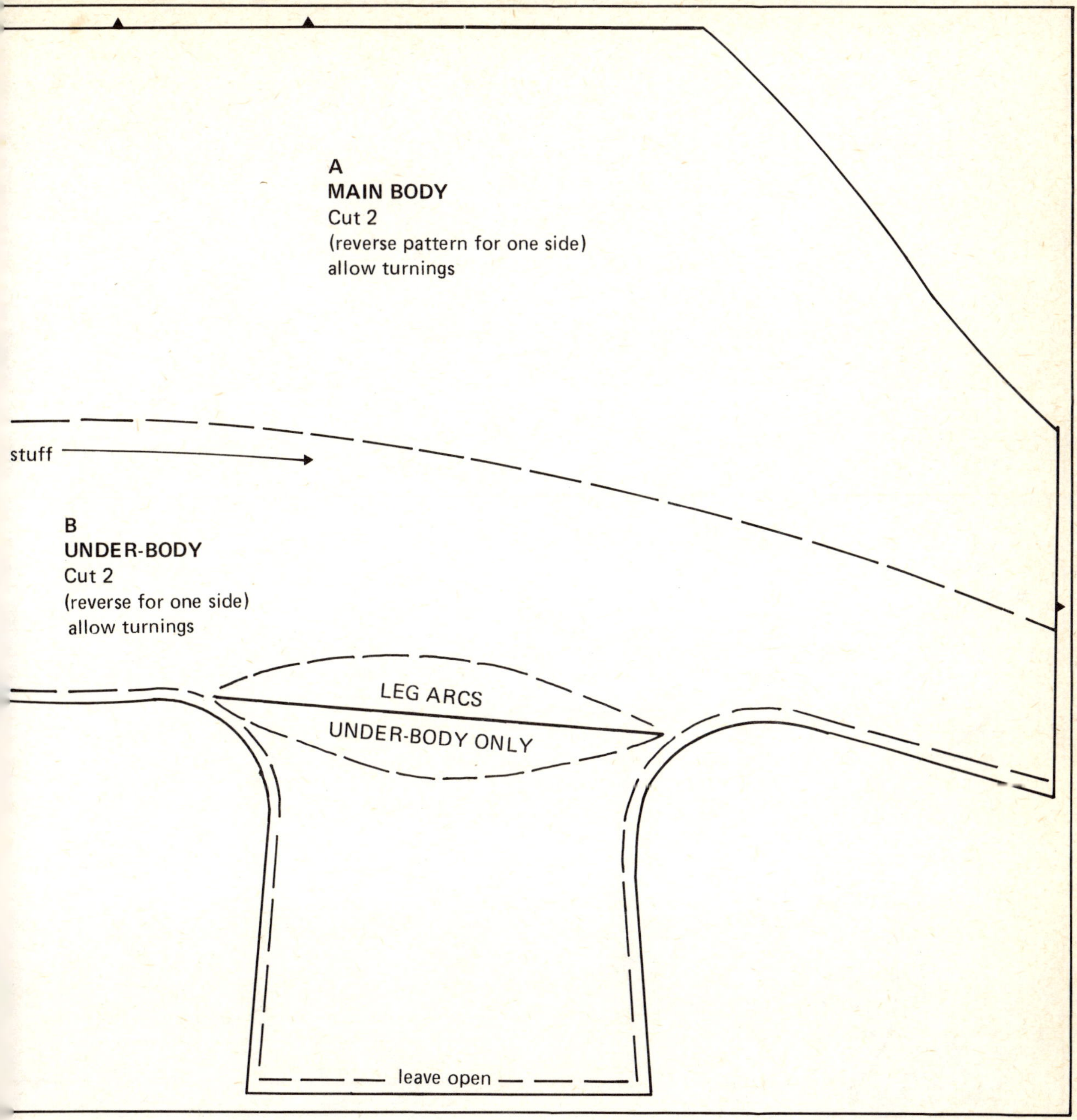

A
MAIN BODY
Cut 2
(reverse pattern for one side)
allow turnings

stuff →

B
UNDER-BODY
Cut 2
(reverse for one side)
 allow turnings

LEG ARCS
UNDER-BODY ONLY

leave open

Head mask

This looks complicated but in fact it goes together very easily.

*Reinforce corners of the horns on all four panels by stay stitching (Fig. 3).

*With right sides together stitch together the centre panels along the centre line, from 'c' at frill edge,

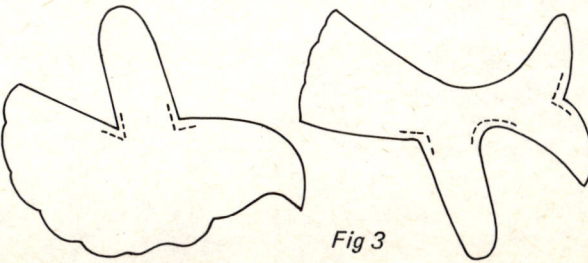

Fig 3

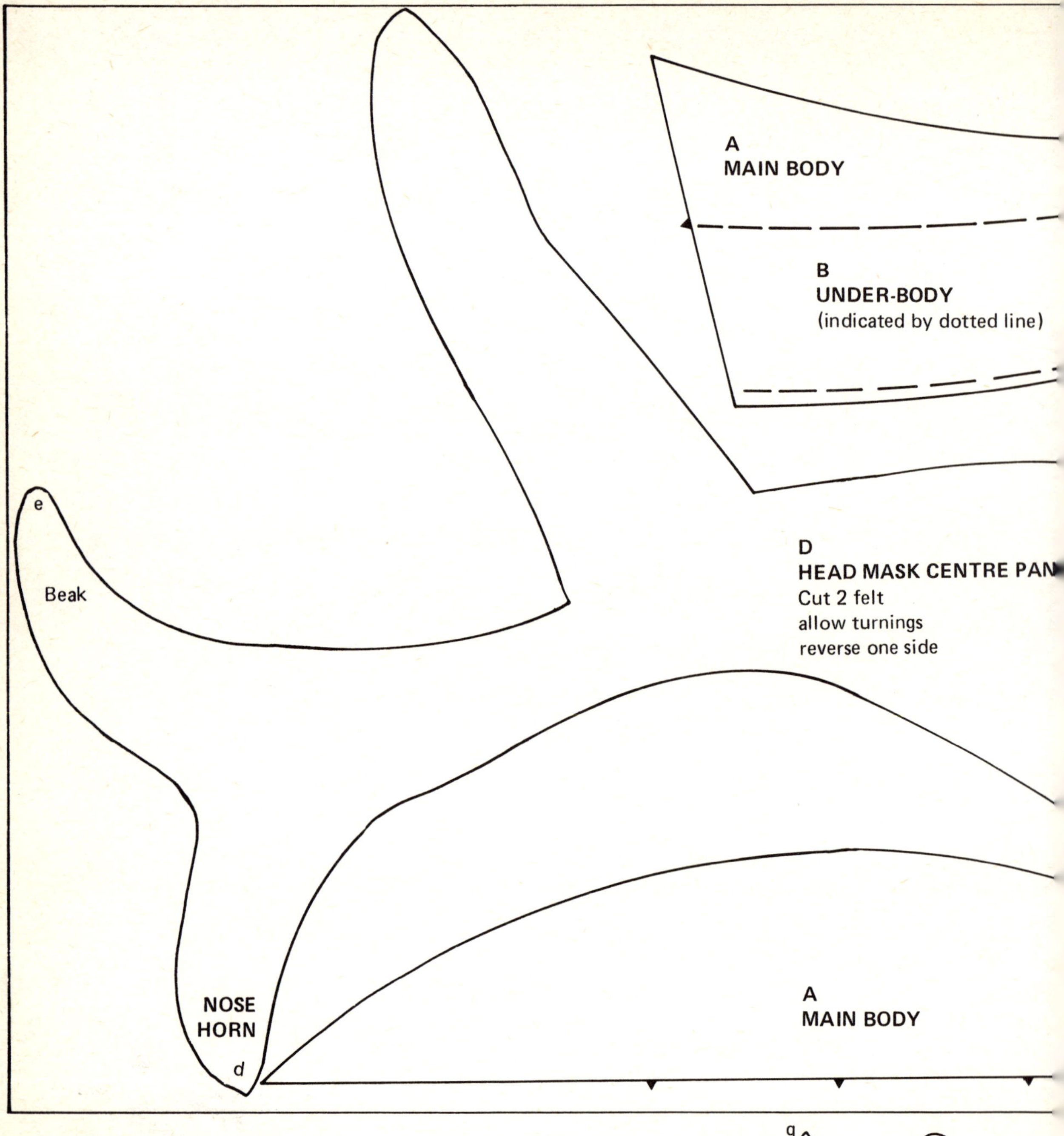

A
MAIN BODY

B
UNDER-BODY
(indicated by dotted line)

D
HEAD MASK CENTRE PAN
Cut 2 felt
allow turnings
reverse one side

e

Beak

NOSE HORN
d

A
MAIN BODY

around nose horn 'd' to the end of the beak 'e' (Fig. 4).

    *With right sides together pin one side panel to one side of joined centre panels, easing where necessary. Stitch from beak 'e' around horn 'f' to edge of frill 'g' (Fig. 5). Repeat for other side. Trim seams and clip curves.

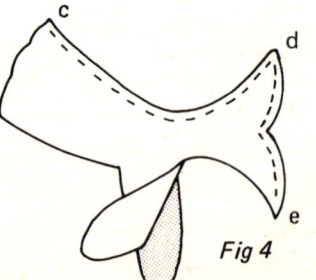

Fig 4

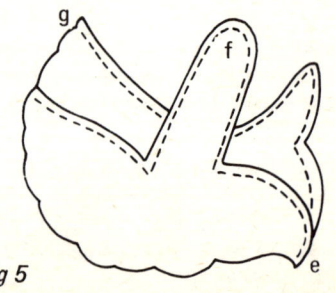

Fig 5

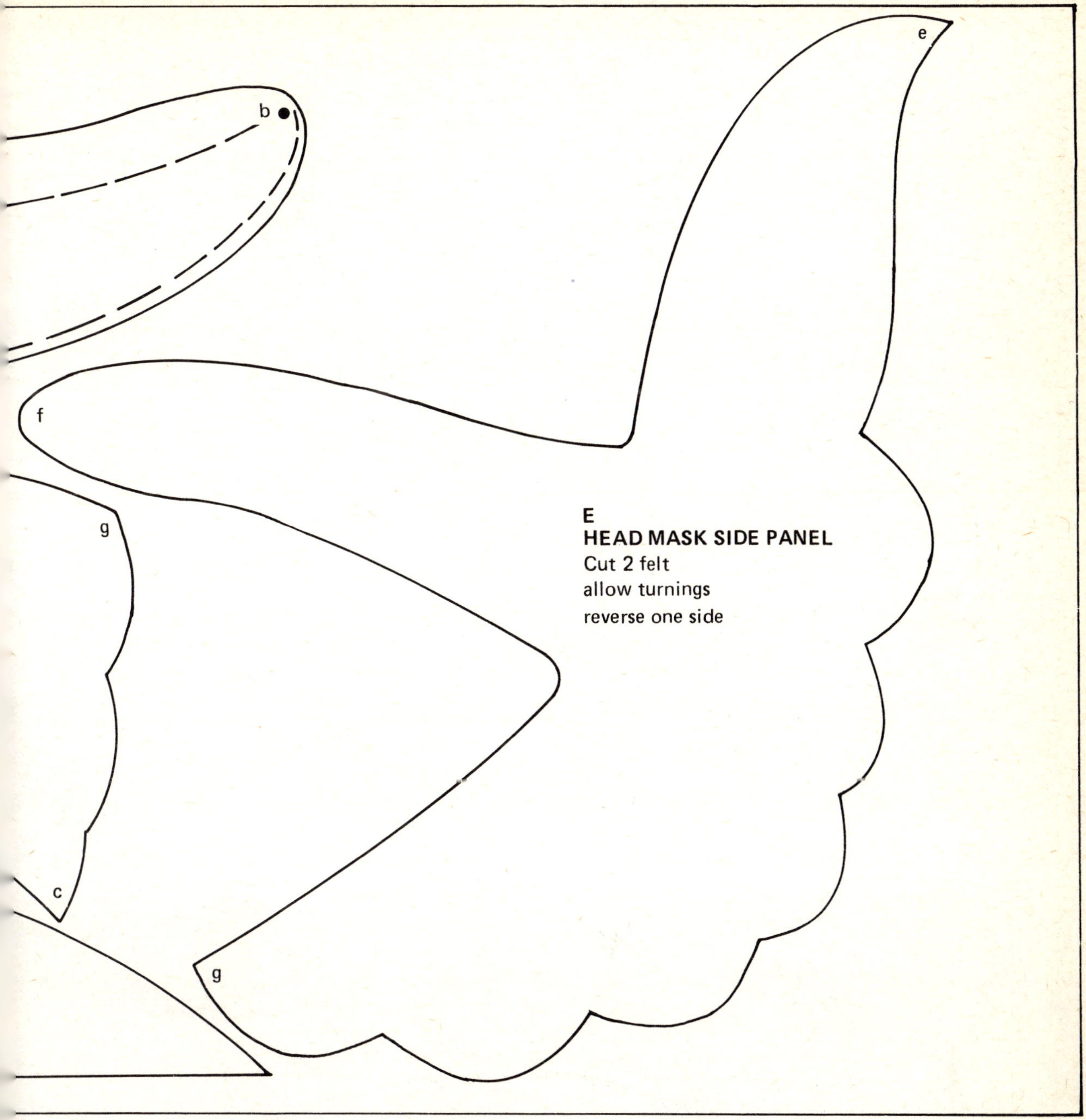

b •

e

f

g

**E
HEAD MASK SIDE PANEL
Cut 2 felt
allow turnings
reverse one side**

c

g

*Stitch frill linings together along centre lines to large dot. Trim seam and press open (Fig. 6).

*With right sides together match scallops and pin frill lining to head mask around the edge.

*Stitch all around scalloped edge and along jaw, beginning and ending at lower edge of beak. Trim seam and clip to scallop curves.

*Turn mask to right side easing out the horns with the blunt end of a knitting needle, and gently pull out the scallops. Turn under frill linings along jaw line and baste into place (Fig. 7). Press edge of mask using a dry cool iron and cloth.

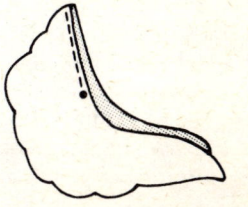

Fig 6

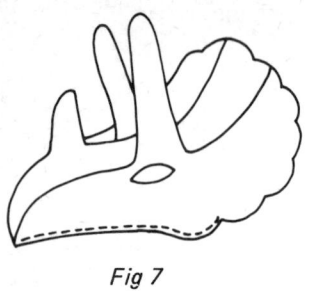

Fig 7

*If plastic eyes are being used, attach these with the eye backings to the top layer of mask only, i.e. NOT through the frill lining. Fix eyes following Hints and Instructions.

*To make under-jaw, stitch two jaw shapes together along one side (Fig. 8) repeat with other two jaw shapes. With right sides together join these two jaw sections together, stitching around edge but leaving open straight edge (Fig. 9). Trim seam turn to right side and press.

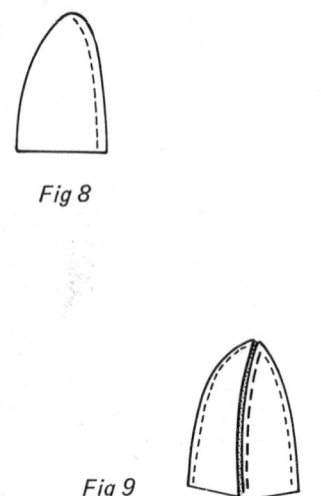

Fig 8

Fig 9

*To attach mask to main body, stuff the horns and beak, place the mask on the body, keep in place with long hat pins or darning needles. A little more stuffing under the mask can be added to make a good shape. Pin under-jaw to chin.

The mask and chin can now be adjusted and more stuffing added if necessary. The beak of a Triceratops is an important feature and should be pulled down to resemble a parrot's beak (Fig. 10).

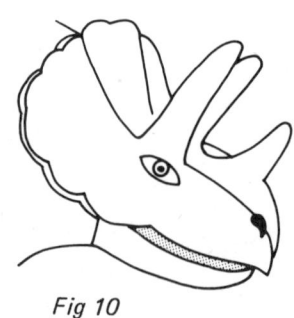

Fig 10

*Slip-stitch mask to head, working along beak and upper jaw line and around frill lining. Take out basting stitches. Slip-stitch lower jaw into place.

*Several stitches can be made through the base of the horns, the stitches passing through felt, fabric and stuffing.

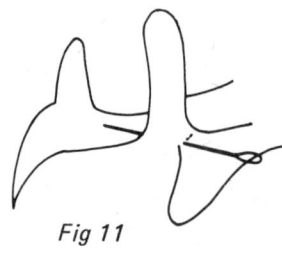

Fig 11

Feet

*Pin and stitch together two foot shapes for each of the four feet. Make a small slit in the top fabric of each foot and insert a little stuffing (Fig. 12).

*Stitch each foot to the ends of the legs which will cover the slits. Three toes are on the front feet, five toes on the back ones.

Fig 12

FINISHING

If plastic eyes have not been used cut a dark eye dot and a slightly larger circle of white felt and stitch these with the eye backing to the head. Stitch or glue the nostrils in position (Fig. 10). The eyelids can now be pinned over the eyes. When you are happy about the expression of the face, slip-stitch the lids in place.

Tyrannosaurus: The King of the Dinosaurs

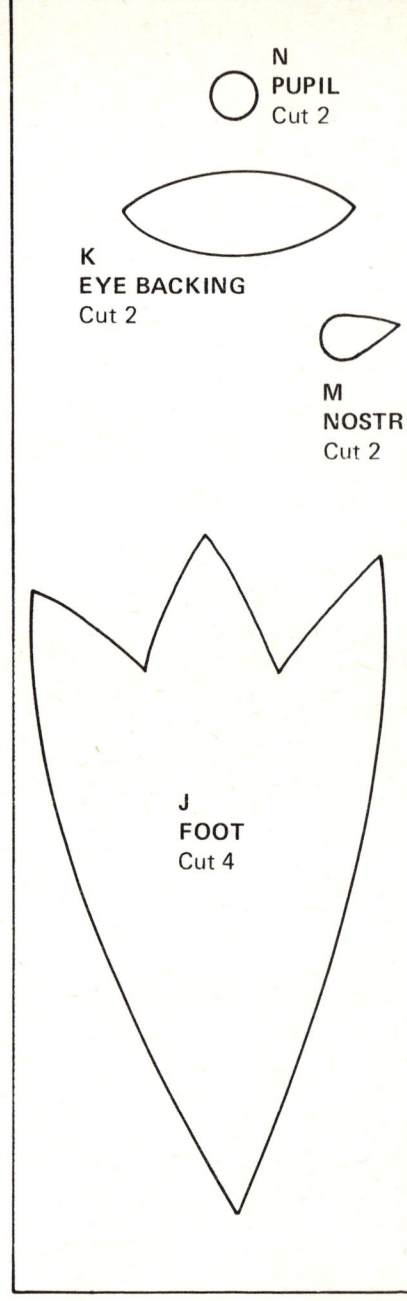

N
PUPIL
Cut 2

K
EYE BACKING
Cut 2

M
NOSTRIL
Cut 2

J
FOOT
Cut 4

Tyrannosaurus (tyrant-lizard) was the largest of the meat-eating dinosaurs and the most terrible animal ever to walk on the earth. It lived in North America during the Cretaceous Period, 100 million years ago. A full-grown tyrannosaur stood 24 feet tall and was 45 feet from head to tail. The strong hind legs had fearful claws, and the body was massive. The forelimbs were tiny and probably quite useless. The head was enormous and furnished with 6 inch long, dagger-like teeth which would have easily killed even the largest of the plant-eaters of the time. Tyrannosaurus, like all the other dinosaurs, became extinct at the end of the Cretaceous Period, 70 million years ago.

MATERIALS REQUIRED

Main body of fabric or felt: 25 x 18ins (60 x 45cm)
Contrast (red) felt: 10 x 10ins (25 x 25cm)
White felt: 8 x 5ins (20 x 12cm)
Green felt jacket: 14 x 9ins (35 x 22cm)
Yellow felt: 2 x 2ins (5 x 5cm)
Scrap black felt
Plastic eyes (optional): 10mm
Sewing cottons
Stuffing: 8oz (226g)
Size of Model: Length 18ins (45 cm); Height 14ins (35cm)

Note: This model is rather smaller than it should be compared to the other designs. However, it is much easier to make at this scale.

MAKING-UP

Patterns

Make-up patterns as explained in Hints and Instructions. Pattern shapes required are: 2 main bodies (A); 1 centre body gusset (B); 2 inner legs (C); 1 head gusset (D); 1 under-tail (E); 4 arms (F); 2 leg circles (G); 1 mouth lining (H); 2 claws (I); 4 feet (J); 2 eye backings (K); 2 rows teeth (L); 2 nostrils (M); 2 eye dots (N).

Cutting out

Lay pattern pieces on to fabrics: 2 main bodies; 1 centre body gusset; 2 inner legs; 1 head gusset; 1 under-tail; 4 arms; 2 leg circles on main body fabric or felt. One mouth lining; 2 claws; 4 feet; 2 eye backings on to contrast felt. Two rows teeth on to white felt. Two nostrils and 2 eye dots on black felt. Note: jacket and pocket in green and yellow felt are dealt with later.

Cut out following Hints and Instructions but do NOT cut along curve of mouth (Fig. 1).

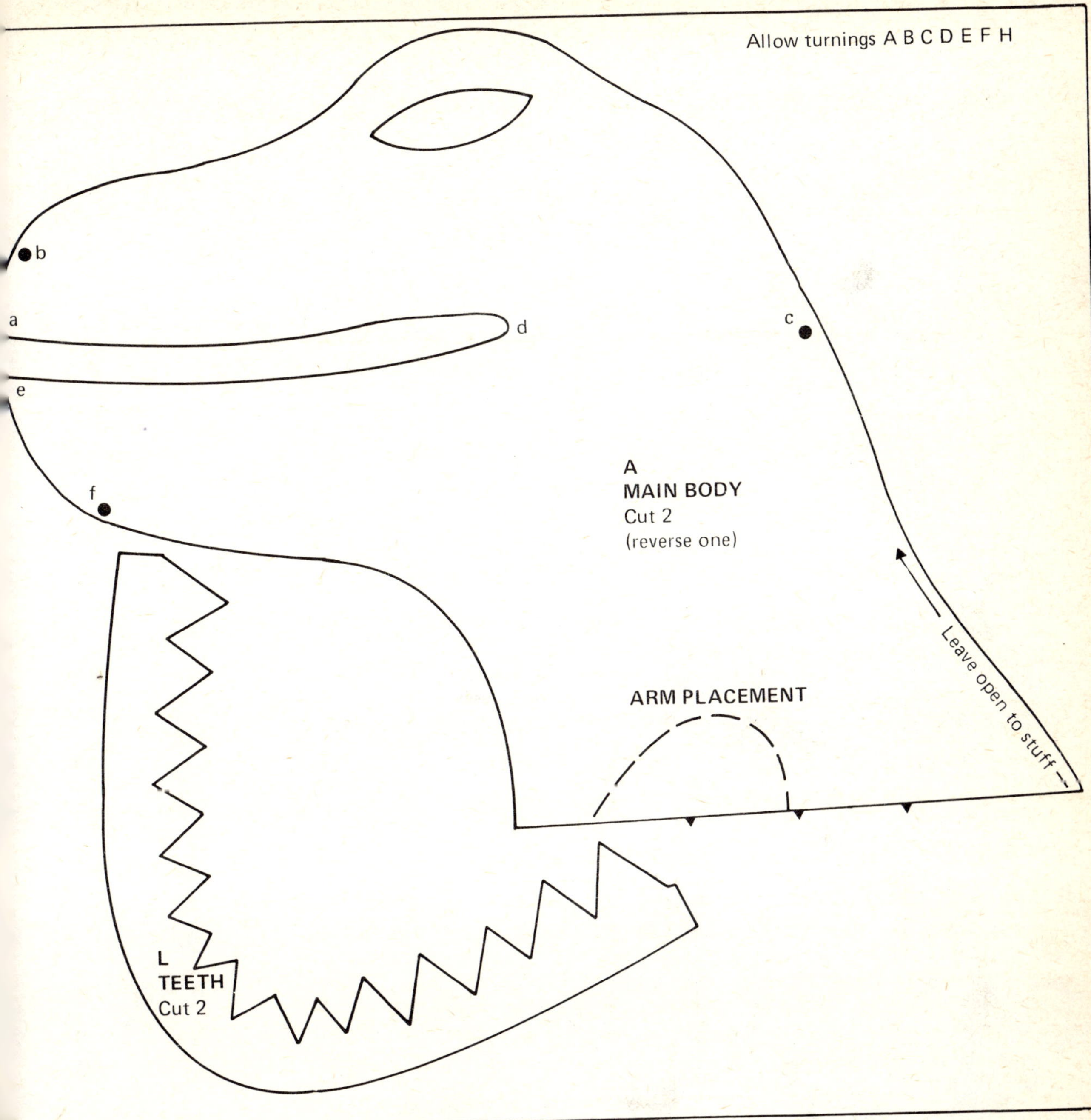

Allow turnings A B C D E F H

b

a

d

e

c

f

A
MAIN BODY
Cut 2
(reverse one)

ARM PLACEMENT

Leave open to stuff →

L
TEETH
Cut 2

Sewing

Main body

*To reinforce mouth and head on each piece, stay-stitch along edge from under the chin, around the mouth line and around the head to back of neck 'c'. Stay-stitch again at corner on mouth 'd' (Fig. 2).

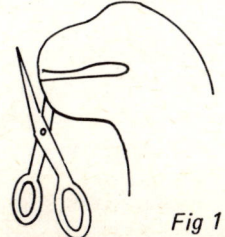

Fig 1

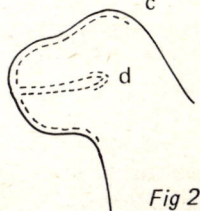

c

d

Fig 2

With right sides together, pin and stitch the two body shapes together at nose and chin 'a'–'b' and 'e'–'f'. Now cut along the centre of the mouth opening between stay-stitching, taking care not to snip stay-stitching at 'd'.

Mouth and teeth

*Pin and baste one row of teeth to each end of mouth lining, on one side of the lining (Fig. 3).

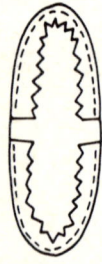

Fig 3

*With teeth to the right side of the body, pin teeth and mouth lining to the mouth opening, easing to fit and snipping corner of mouth at 'd' if necessary. Stitch carefully to the edge at 'd', breaking stitching at 'a' and 'e' (Fig. 4).

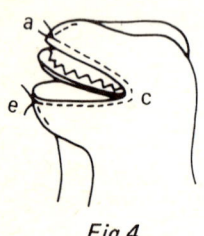

Fig 4

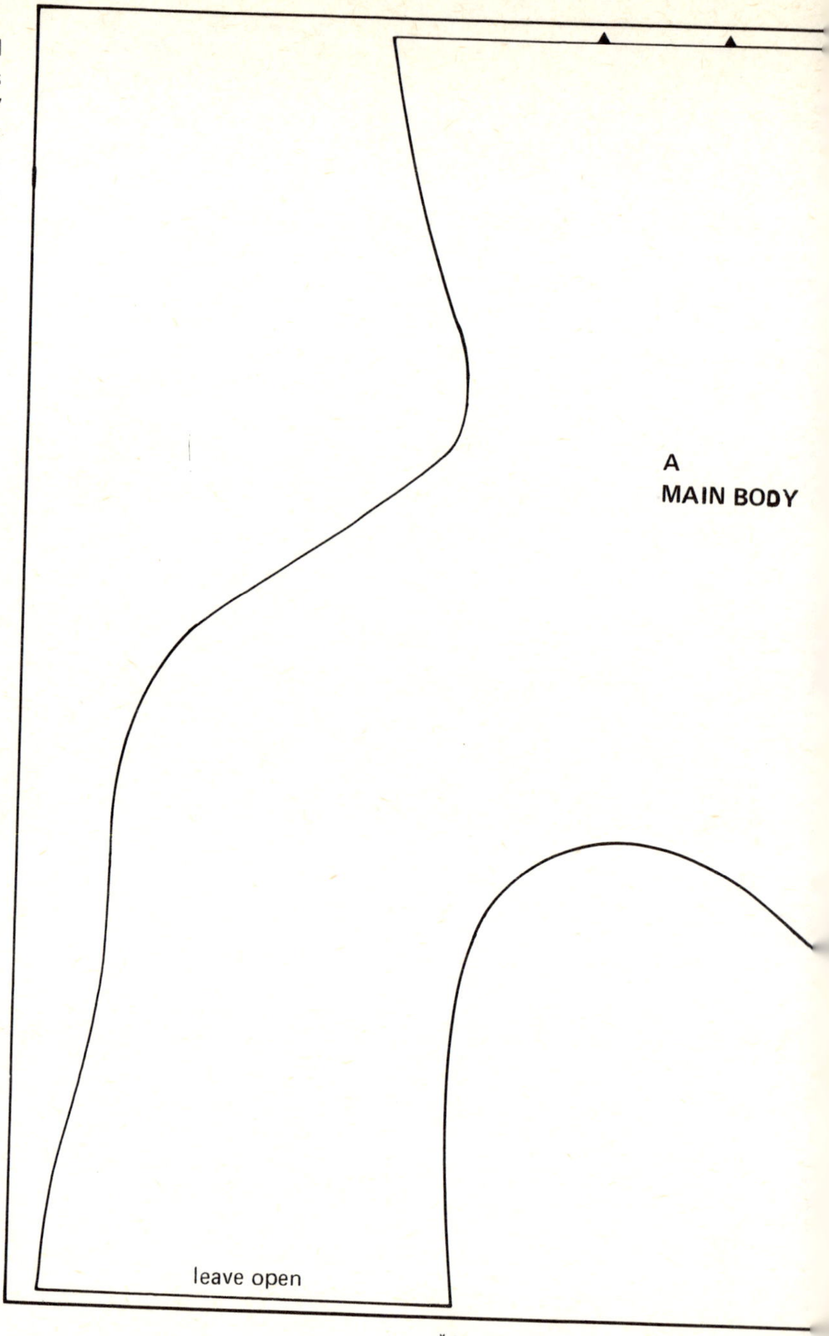

*With right sides together, insert head gusset by stitching from nose 'b' to neck 'c' on one side of head. Repeat for other side (Fig. 5).

*If a plastic safety eye is to be used, turn the head to right side, pin the eye backing in place and insert eyes following Hints and Instructions.

A
MAIN BODY

leave open

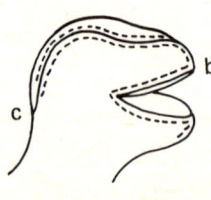

Fig 5

*Stitch together centre back seam from 'c' to 'g' at tail, leaving open gap for stuffing (Fig. 6).

*Stitch inner legs to centre body gusset matching 'k' and 'l' and join under-tail to centre gusset matching 'h' and 'j' (Fig. 7).

*With right sides together, pin complete centre gusset and under-

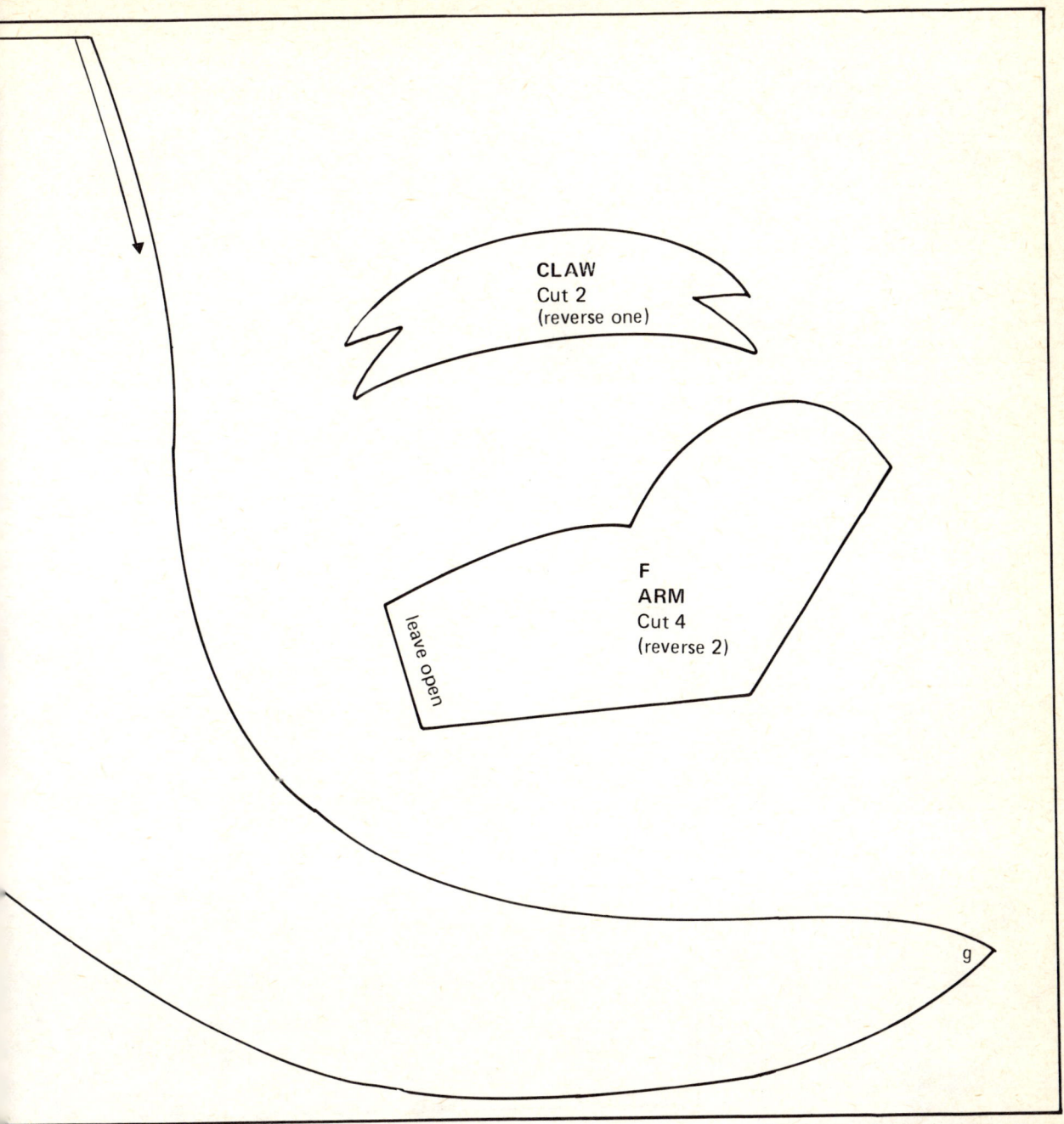

CLAW
Cut 2
(reverse one)

F
ARM
Cut 4
(reverse 2)

leave open

g

tail to main bodies from 'f' under chin to 'g' at end of tail. Ease under-tail to fit curve. Stitch one side of gusset, leaving open the end of the leg. Repeat for other side of body. Trim seams and clip to curve.

*Insert leg circles and stitch by hand, trimming to size and oversewing if felt is used (see Hints and Instructions).

*Check that no pins are left in the fabric, turn the Tyrannosaurus to right side out easing out the jaw and tail with the stick.

Stuffing

*Fill the Tyrannosaurus with stuffing, beginning with the head and jaw and carefully moulding the stuffing into the head. Take care while stuffing that the inner seam of the mouth is pressed against the body fabric, the teeth will then point upwards and downwards. Fill the legs and tail well. The creature will balance and stand perfectly if the filling is smooth and firm. If a larger model is to be made, an arch of wire can be inserted before the body filling is completed (Fig. 8). Complete stuffing and close the gap in the back. Brush to remove excess filling.

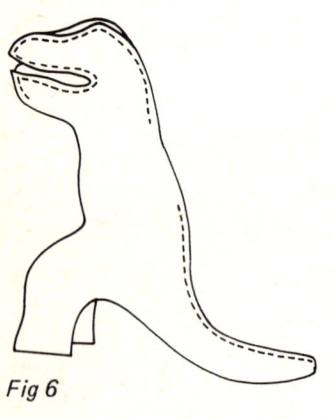

Fig 6

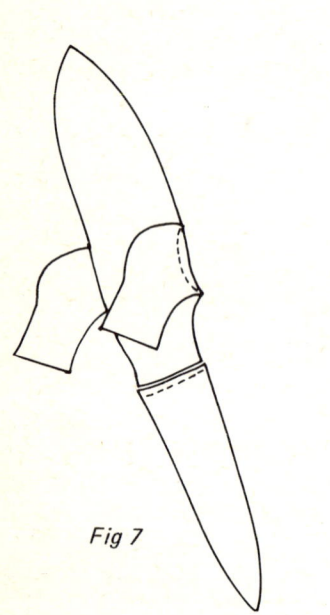

Fig 7

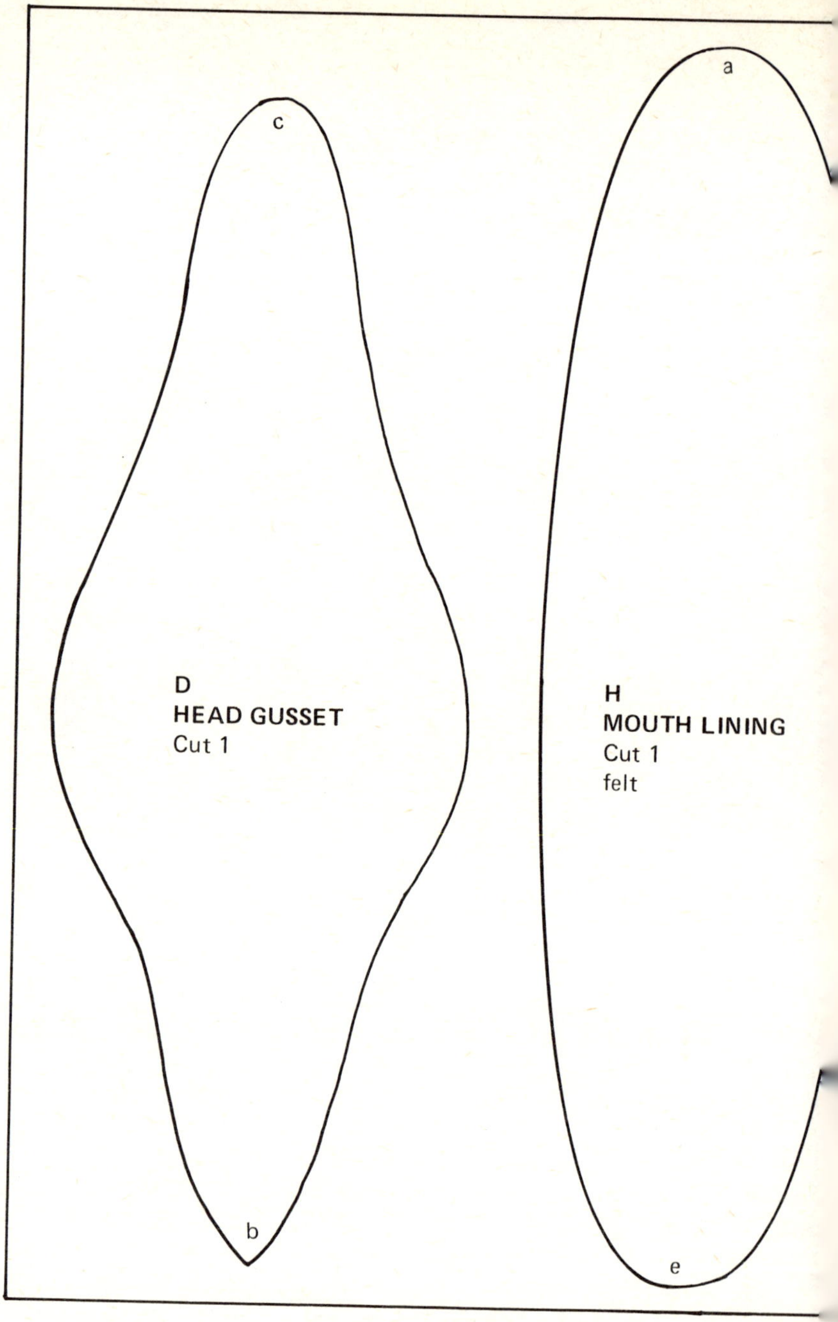

D
HEAD GUSSET
Cut 1

c

b

H
MOUTH LINING
Cut 1
felt

a

e

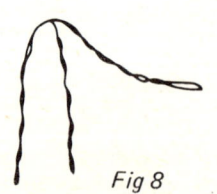

Fig 8

Arms

*Pin and stitch two arm shapes together, leaving open straight edge (Fig. 9). Trim seam, turn to right side and fill with stuffing.

*Each claw is folded in half and top stitched or oversewn close to the edge.

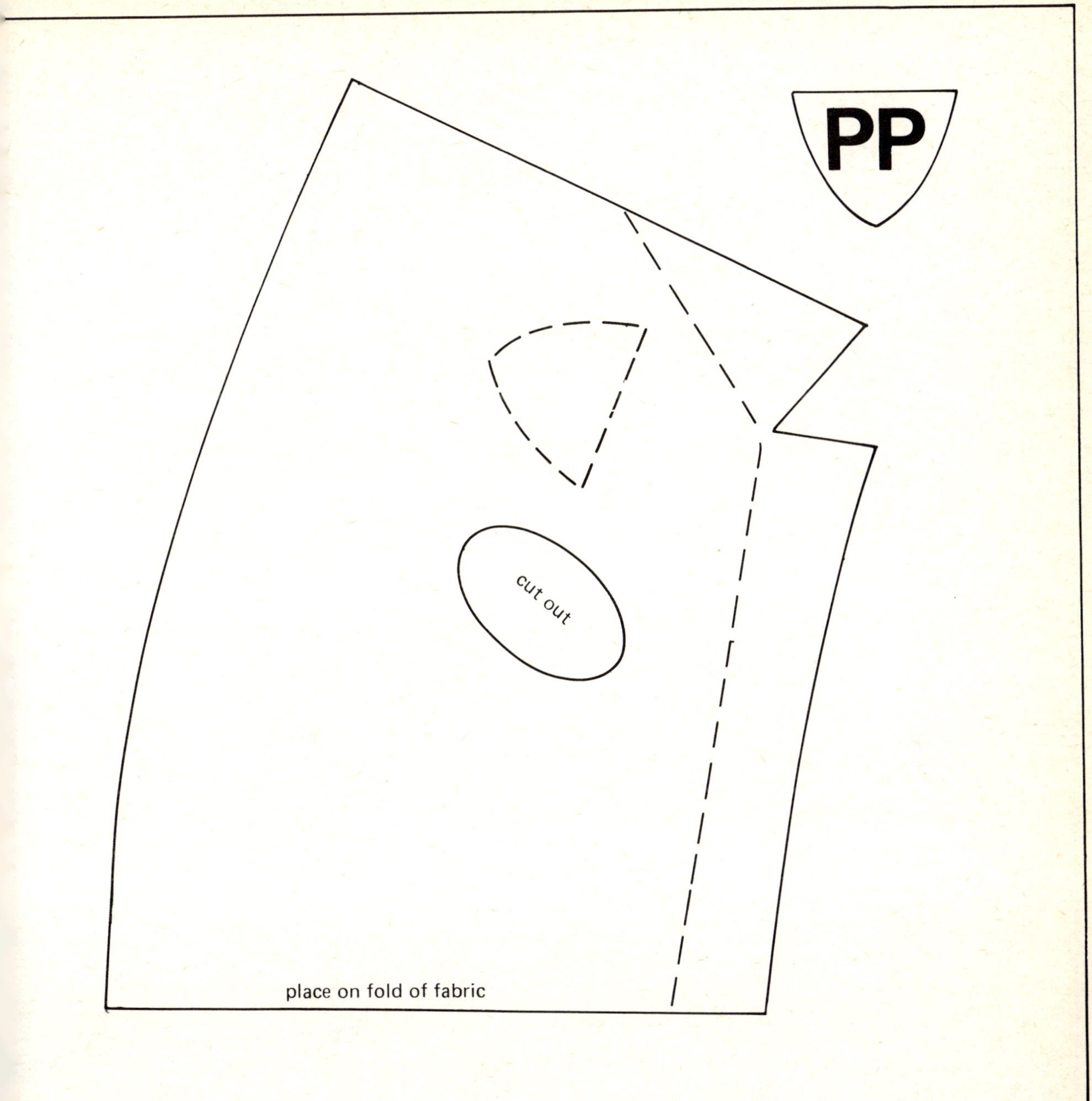

PP

cut out

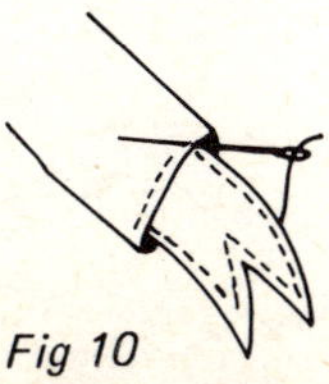

place on fold of fabric

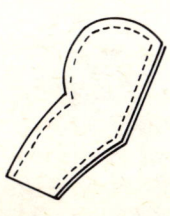

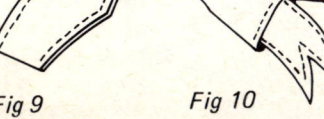

*Turn under raw edge of arm, insert claw and stab-stitch in place (Fig. 10).

*Stitch arm to body. Repeat for second arm.

Feet

*Top stitch two foot shapes together. Make a small cross slit in the top fabric only and insert a little filling (Fig. 11). Repeat for other foot.

*Stitch feet to ends of legs (Fig. 12).

Fig 9   Fig 10

Fig 11

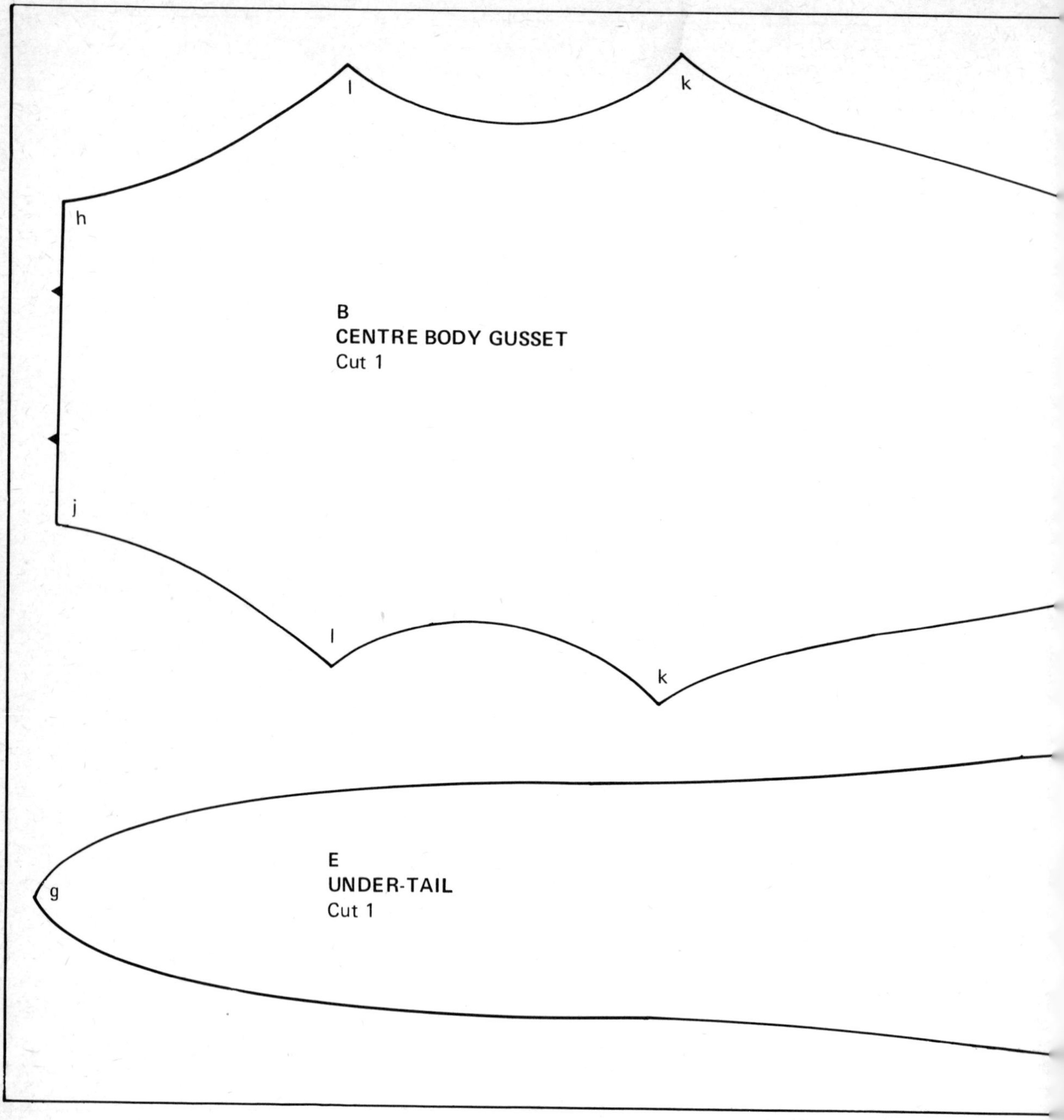

l
k
h
B
CENTRE BODY GUSSET
Cut 1
j
l
k
E
UNDER-TAIL
Cut 1
g

Fig 12

Finishing

*If plastic eyes have not been used, cut out two small dots from black felt and two slightly larger circles from white felt. Stitch these on top of the eye backing to the head. Stitch or glue two nostrils in place (Fig. 13).

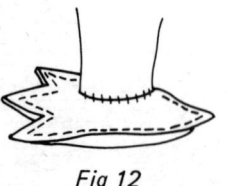

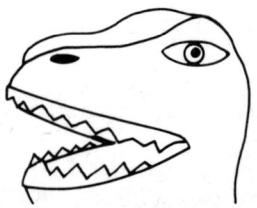

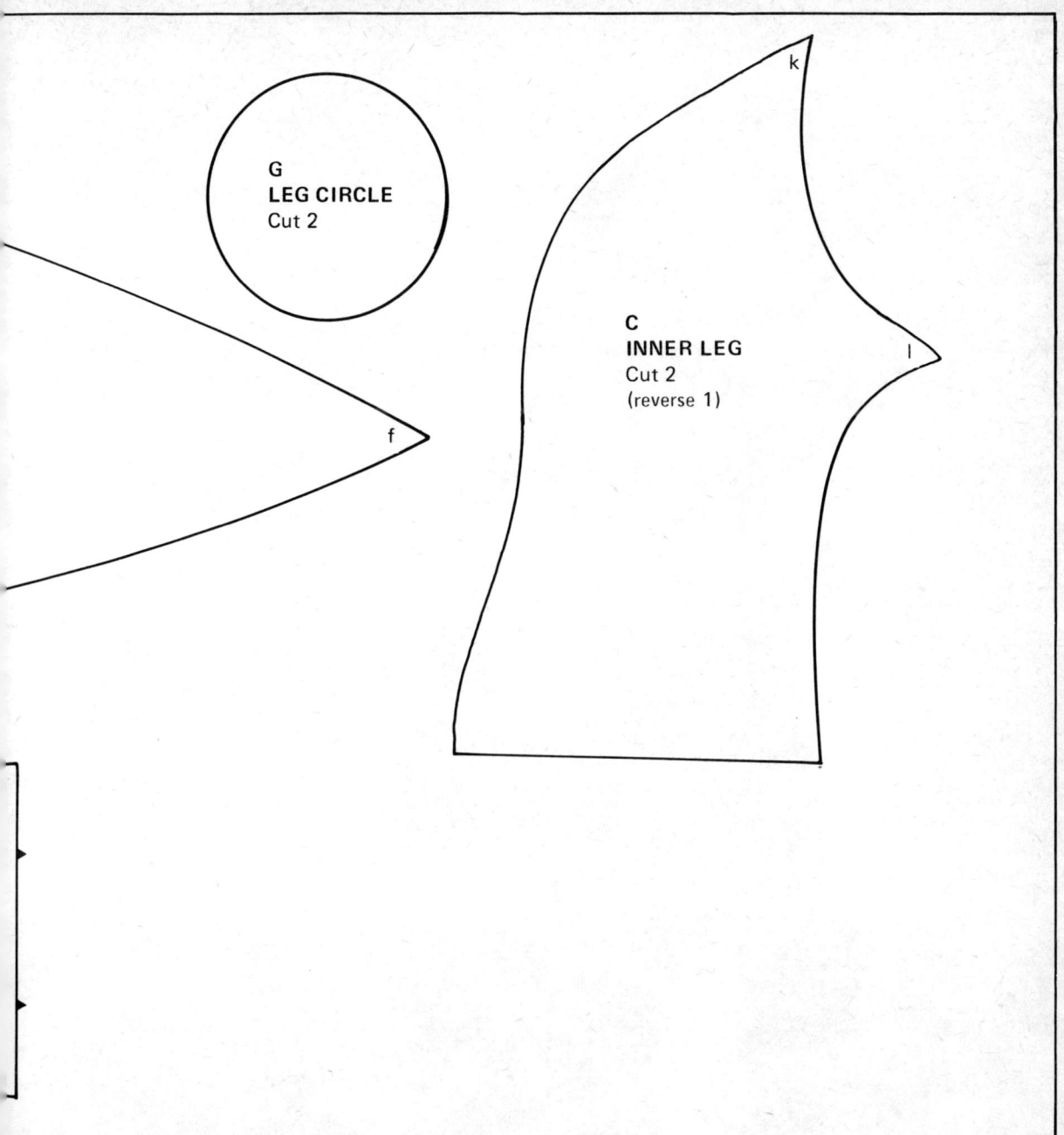

G
LEG CIRCLE
Cut 2

C
INNER LEG
Cut 2
(reverse 1)

f

k

l

Jacket

*Cut the jacket shape from green felt and the pocket from yellow felt.

*Press down the collar and revers of the jacket. Stitch the pocket in position and fit on the jacket.